Looking In, Looking Out, Looking Up

Best Wishes Dale—Sharm Brundtu—Brew

all the best always, Roger & Brewer

Karen Bergenholtz wishing you all life's
Blessings, always

Peace + love to you— Millie

Thank you for everything
Paul Bergenholtz

love ya, Bridget

with Thanksgiving for your
leadership and God's blessing
to you and your family in all
your future endeavors,
Valerie

Sending you off
with all our love!
♡ Eric Michund

Looking In, Looking Out, Looking Up

REFLECTIONS FROM THE
MFC DEACONS

Photo by Carmen B. Roundtree

Deacons of the Middlefield Federated Church

ISBN-13: 9781535119443
ISBN-10: 1535119446

Contents

Acknowledgements

THANKS TO JUDI RAND THE church's secretary who saved all the old *Red Doors* and made it very easy for me (the compiler of these reflections) to locate many of the earlier writings.

Thanks to all the other deacons, past and present, for allowing me to go ahead with the project. They helped in so many different ways, especially by their inspiring reflections.

Thanks to Roger and Nicole, my husband and daughter, who tolerated my craziness, my questions to them, and my need for them to affirm the choices I made as I put this book together.

Thanks to all the laity of our church who inspire the deacons to serve with them. Together we continue to fulfill our church's mission: *"With the help of the Holy Spirit, our Mission is to build and strengthen relationships with God, one another, and our world."*

Introduction

I HAVE TO CONFESS THAT when I read nonfiction books, I don't always read the introduction to those books because I want to dive right into what I consider the meat of the book. Sometimes I read the introduction later, but many times I don't read it at all, especially if it is long. Having said that, I hope you read this introduction because it will give you some important information about this book, and it will introduce you to the people who wrote what is in this book (the deacons of the Middlefield Federated church), and it will introduce you to the church where we all "build and strengthen relationships with God, one another, and the world."

As specified in the Articles of Federation of the Middlefield Federated Church, the deacons of this church do not manage budget, staff, property, or other administrative matters. The Visionary Board is the governing body of the church. The deacons are spiritual leaders of the church and, along with the Pastor, try to attend to the spiritual needs of the congregation.

The Middlefield Federated Church is a two-denominational church. In 1921, The Middlefield Congregational Church (now a member of the United Church of Christ) and the Middlefield United Methodist Church joined together in common work and worship under the name of the Middlefield Federated Church.

Prior to 2003, there were no deacons of the Middlefield United Methodist Church or the Middlefield Federated Church. At that time, the Middlefield Congregational Church had deacons, but they handled only a few ceremonial tasks. In 2003, the Middlefield Federated Church established its own active well-defined Board of Deacons. The Middlefield Congregational Church therefore had no further use for its deacons and eliminated its Board of Deacons altogether. Ten years later, in 2013, the Middlefield Federated Church restructured its organization and eliminated all boards and committees. The deacons continued to function as established in 2003 but now became known as the Deacons or the Deacon group.

It has been my privilege to serve as a deacon of the Middlefield Federated Church since 2003. As deacons, we nurture our faith through study and prayer and by working with each other and the Pastor. We initiate and facilitate different programs to help nourish the congregation, programs such as *Unwrapping Our Gifts, Sweet Hour of Prayer,* and *Faith Forum.* We participate with the Pastor in leading worship by taking on different parts of the worship service as deacon liturgist. We serve the congregation (sometimes leading worship) during the Pastor's absence. We mentor in the confirmation of youth and provide training for new church members. We assist with baptisms and communion. We serve home communion and visit those who are sick or shut-in. As deacons, we strive to be as visible and as available to the congregation as needed. We always make an effort to be a presence at church functions. And, since 2003, the deacons have also been writing, on a rotating schedule, devotional articles for publication in our church newsletter, the *Red Doors,* which is now published on a monthly basis. A total of 150 articles have been written and published since 2003.

Recently, I found myself reading a number of the deacons' past articles from the *Red Doors.* I had no particular purpose in mind when I started re-reading these past articles. I was reading them as a matter of interest and curiosity. However, as I was reading, I was totally and thoroughly impressed with the content and emotion in so many of the articles. For one thing, the articles reminded me of various past programs, projects, and initiatives of the deacons and of the church overall. For example, many of the articles contain testimony about mission work, such as trips to Haiti to help build a medical clinic and trips to Mississippi to help those who suffered as a result of hurricane Katrina. In addition, the articles speak of incidences and events in our community, country, and the wider world that had an impact on each of us in the church in some way. But what impressed me most about the articles was the deep genuine sharing of personal beliefs and stories. I was touched and fed by the committed individuals sharing their faith journeys.

As I reflected on the past articles written by our deacons, it occurred to me that it might be a good idea to combine all the articles written by deacons (past and present) into a single publication and make this publication available to the congregation and perhaps to others who may have an interest. I took the idea to the deacon group and got permission to proceed with the project.

We, the deacons of the Middlefield Federated Church, are not professional writers. We have not been formally trained or educated in theology. Moreover, the articles in this book were not written for book publication. Other than, for privacy reasons, using initials for the people mentioned in the articles who were not deacons, I have not tried to enhance the articles by editing them. Plainly and simply, we are lay people sharing from the heart, and I did not want to alter the original writings to detract from that.

I get great personal satisfaction in serving with the deacons of our church. We each have different gifts that enable us to contribute to the congregation and to our brothers and sisters around the world. Some of us are gifted at delivering messages. Some of us are gifted at home visitation or facilitating programs. Some of us are gifted in maintaining good personal relationships. Whatever our gifts, we work together and with the rest of the congregation enhancing the role of the laity in our church, in the community, and in the wider world with hopes of bringing about a world of love and peace.

It is my wish that you will be inspired, guided, and fed in some significant and meaningful way by the reflections in this book just as I have been. I hope that you are touched. I hope that you are encouraged. I hope that you are motivated. I hope that you appreciate how the deacons have reached deep within to enrich themselves and to benefit others.

Sharon Roundtree-Brewer

2003

Trying New Wings
Dorothy Waller

THE DEACONS ELECTED IN FEBRUARY are still meeting monthly, still reading and discussing Philip Yancey's book *The Jesus I Never Knew*, (which, by the way, is a very insightful and sensitive book), and still finding those areas where we can be most supportive of the Pastor and the church as a whole. With a congregation of this size, the demands on the Pastor's time are constant, as we all know. How to relieve him of or assist him in, some of his regular activities, becomes a part of our discussion at each meeting. And you are looking at one of the ways that we feel we can help.

The Pastor has regularly written a first-page article for the *Red Doors* with each publication, and the deacons are going to take the responsibility for the article EVERY OTHER mailing. Lots of other ideas are percolating, as well. How do we become a more Bible-familiar congregation; how do we more effectively reach out to the needs of the greater Middlefield/Rockfall/Durham/Middletown community; how do we offer opportunities for dialogue when common concerns arise (i.e. September 11, or the war in Iraq). How do we keep a sense of humor as our physical church disintegrates around us? We are starting to address the needs of our shut-ins by regular visits, accompanying the Pastor. At least one of the deacons will be present for weddings, funeral services and baptisms. There are loads of areas where we can and will be available — we are just beginning to try our new wings. We pray that we will be moving in the right direction.

Happy New Year (I)

Sue VanDerzee

▲ ▲ ▲

HAPPY NEW YEAR!

WELL, MAYBE NOT REALLY HAPPY NEW YEAR, but it certainly does feel like that each September as our church family "comes home" to Middlefield. This year, of course, coming home is a bit different as we worship across the street in the Middlefield Community Center. As the Pastor pointed out on the first Sunday in our temporary home, however, the church is more than a building—much more.

That has particular relevance to the deacons as we attempt to hammer out a role and help provide spiritual direction in a growing congregation.

While we are reading our way through *The Jesus I Never Knew* for our own spiritual nourishment, we have also considered in what ways we can help nourish the congregation and the Pastor. One of the ways, as Deacon Dorothy Waller pointed out last month, is to remove the burden of producing two front pages for the *Red Doors* each month from the Pastor. Another is by helping him with visitations.

One of the ways we would like to help nourish the congregation is through hosting what we are calling "Faith Forums." We figure we'd like to present four to six of these a year, focusing on questions of "real life" and how our faith might impact those areas. These are not areas that we expect to agree on, even as a Board of Deacons. On the contrary, they raise questions that challenge and confound us as Christians and disciples during the beginning of the 21st century. Our first faith forum will be Wednesday, October 22, at

7:30 PM and the topic will be "Separation of Church and State." A discussion starter article will be available for anyone interested in this topic to read beforehand if they wish. (Homework is optional, however!)

The questions we considered in our deacons' discussion last month were inspired by our continuing readings and concerned the issues of Holy Week and the Resurrection. One provocative subject concerned Jesus' washing of his disciples' feet during celebration of the Passover meal. We considered how that would make us feel today and why this is not a usual practice despite our denominations' attempts to "do as Jesus did." Differing cultures was cited as perhaps the reason that the subject is uncomfortable for American Christians in 2003. What do you think?

The second major discussion topic concerned doubt and faith, and how they relate to one another. We mostly found ourselves echoing the sentiment of the disciple who said to Jesus: "Lord, I believe. Help thou my unbelief."

As we start this "new year," let us help each other wrestle with the great questions that our status as followers of Jesus poses to us.

The First Faith Forum

Karen Bergenholtz

▲ ▲ ▲

FRIENDS, ROMANS, COUNTRYMEN, LEND ME your ears!
Oops, scratch that first line; let's try again.

Dear Friends in Christ,

Ah yes, much better. It is my privilege to invite all to the first "FAITH FORUM" instigated by the deacons here at Middlefield Federated Church.

The first topic proposed for discussion is "Separation of Church and State," certainly an elusive subject which many of us tread carefully through, and around. How do we as Christians respond to questions concerning church/state relationships? Not sure? – That makes two of us, at least! And that is one reason we offer "FAITH FORUM", as an avenue of exploring our beliefs and faith, as individuals and in community.

Where to begin? Perhaps consider how we arrive at our beliefs on moral issues, which concern all of society. Personal experiences, family tradition, media, etc. influence us. As Christians, though, how do we discern how God would have us think/act regarding certain issues, such as the death penalty, or euthanasia?

The article the Pastor has offered as a springboard explains John Wesley's "four tools for discerning God's will." Wesley lays out four tools: scripture, tradition of church, experience of the Holy Spirit at work in our lives, and our God-given ability to reason. We encourage all to utilize these four tools at the FAITH FORUM in discussion of how we as Christians strive to live in right relationship with God, and in turn, influence our society in positive ways. Now if these four tools seem heavy, we also will learn from each other, as we search our hearts and minds.

If you don't know where to start, consider the recent news of a Ten Commandment monument's removal from the Alabama State Judicial building, the removal mandated by a U.S. District judge. Do you think the monument belonged there, or not?

We offer the article, which the Pastor provided us with for your perusal and thoughtfulness. Articles will be available as you enter church at the Community Center on Sundays.

Talking About Our Faith

Sharon Roundtree-Brewer

▲ ▲ ▲

AS YOU HAVE BEEN READING on this page of the *Red Doors*, the Board of Deacons is hosting monthly discussions called the Faith Forum. Our first forum was held on Tuesday, October 28 at 7:30 p. m. in the Education Building. The topic of the night was The Separation of Church and State, and the first chapter of Adam Hamilton's book, *Confronting the Controversies: A Christian Looks at the Tough Issues*, was used as a framework for our conversation.

The discussion was not designed to reach any resolution on the issue or to establish any consensus. The forum was designed to give people an opportunity to talk about contemporary issues from the perspective of their faith and to hear what others had to say about these issues. The small but willing group offered stimulating conversation with diverse opinions. As we discussed the pros and cons of separating church and state, we moved into other interesting topics that included what Christians can do to reach out to others to bring them into the faith community.

What struck me that evening was the fact that although the participants in the discussion had different views and expressed them in quite different ways, each person was clearly thinking about life and life's issues from a position of faith. I was quite impressed by the strength and clarity with which some expressed where they stood on certain issues, but thought that there must have been others such as I still wrestling with the nuances of these types of issues and thus benefiting immensely from the discussion. As I listened to the conversations (I must admit I did more listening than talking) it occurred to me that most of us were at different points in our personal faith journey, and the fact that we were at different points influenced how we viewed the issues. What also struck me was that although there were areas of disagreement, we listened to the ideas and comments of our fellow sojourners with respect and open-mindedness. I felt that God was speaking to me through the voices of those present. Perhaps others felt the same.

The next Faith Forum will be Tuesday, December 2, 2003 at 7:30 p.m., in the Education Building. The group that assembled that evening has chosen the topic of euthanasia for this discussion. We hope that you will be able to attend and have an opportunity to share your faith.

With the trust that we always act with God's spirit, love, and understanding in our hearts, be well.

DECEMBER 15

What is Our Vision for MFC?

Richard Kennedy

VISION: Something seen in the mind; unusual ability to think or plan ahead.

I RECENTLY TOURED OUR NEW BUILDING and was quite impressed. The rooms are beginning to take shape, walls are up, and the altar is huge! What a beautiful place it is going to be to meet, have fellowship and bring our Christian family together to do God's work!

It has been a long and sometimes trying two plus years. We started with a dream, made it a goal and with a lot of work, time and energy soon that goal was realized. This dream or vision brought us together as a family and with our vision ever present we worked as a team to make it happen. Now what?

What is our vision for our church? The Church is not the building, but the people in it. What does the church family want this building to represent to the community? What do we want to do as a church body? What does God want MFC to do?

The Board of Deacons feels it is important for the church's spiritual well being to develop a vision for our church as we enter our new building. This vision will be our direction in how we further God's work in Middlefield and the world. With this in mind we propose that the church family initiate the visioning process early in 2004. The Deacons would ask you to begin thinking about your vision for our church and prepare to share it as we embark on this new journey, that of developing a vision for the Middlefield Federated Church family in our new home. Look for further information to come soon.

On behalf of the Board of Deacons we wish you a joyous Christmas season. May it bring you God's peace and love.

2004

Prayer For the New Year

Roger Brewer

▲ ▲ ▲

FREQUENTLY, THOUGH PROBABLY NOT AS OFTEN as I should, I sit quietly and try to name all the blessings that God has brought into my life and give thanks for each and every one. I find this type of prayer especially helpful when I'm disappointed by a certain development or occurrence or when I encounter specific difficulties or tribulations. By giving thanks for my blessings, I am able to regain the proper perspective in my life. I am reminded that despite my perception of present circumstances God is always with me. I also like to identify and give thanks for my blessings during the final days of each calendar year. It helps me to assess the overall developments in my life and determine priorities for the following year.

I sat quietly this New Year's Eve giving thanks to God for my physical, mental, emotional and spiritual health. I gave thanks for the health of my family and my friends. I gave thanks for the comfort and personal achievement brought forth into my life. I gave thanks for the love, trust, commitment, and overall health I enjoy in my personal relationships with others, including my wife, my children, my brothers and sisters and their children, my church family, my friends, my co-workers, members of my community and those special people who enter my life and touch me in special ways. I gave thanks also for the health, strength and goodness in those many personal relationships that have certainly developed within and among the members of our church family. I believe these relationships are precious treasures that make our congregation strong. I continue to give thanks and pray that these relationships may continue to grow and prosper and nourish us according to our needs.

I have continued since my prayer on New Year's Eve to give special thanks for the health and vitality in the relationships within our congregation. Among my hopes and prayers for the year 2004 is the prayer that we may continue as a church to build and sustain significant personal relationships. Though we come from various backgrounds and perhaps hold diverse opinions on political, social and economic issues, we build relationships as we worship and work together, as we share our faith journeys, as we care for each other and as we participate together in fellowship activities. As stated in 1 John 4, verses 7 and 12, "Beloved, let us love one another because love is from God…if we love one another, God lives in us, and his love is perfected in us."

And Now What?

Dorothy Waller

THERE IS A PHRASE IN THE BOOK OF AMOS that deserves our attention. Amos was a minor Old Testament prophet. He was a shepherd who was used by God in the 8th century B.C. to speak to the Israelites who were going their own way and not living up to God's expectations of them. The phrase that Amos used was, "Woe to those who are at ease in Zion and to those who feel secure in the mountains of Samaria. Apparently things were going along rather well for the Israelites and they began to feel complacent, taking their good times for granted.

This is a phrase we should all keep before us, lest we sink into complacency after the enormous effort put into the building process. That, plus our relatively comfortable lives makes it very easy to do. We look around at the church renovation and can truly say, "Wow, we've done a great thing! Aren't we terrific?" And we HAVE done a good thing, and we ARE terrific! And it will be very easy to sit back and feel good about ourselves.

But it is just at this time that we need to ask God for direction, for a purpose—for ourselves and for this building. It wasn't built just to look at and admire, or to serve just ourselves. Now is the time to begin to find out how God wants us to use this building, and how to focus our gifts and talents—so that we may truly become what we are called to be—the BODY OF CHRIST, to carry out the work of God.

The deacons are currently discussing ways by which we, as a church, can go through a "Visioning" process. Once we have found a process that we think will work, we will train ourselves, and perhaps others, to take us all, young and old alike, through this "Visioning" approach. In the meantime, we should ALL be thinking of what we want our church to be and do.

God, through Amos, sent a warning to the Israelites, saying that judgment was coming because of our complacency. And punishment followed. Now, I don't expect our punishment to be capture and exile if we maintain the status quo. But we WOULD miss out on the joy that we will experience if we feel that this is a beginning, a start of new life within our church. Already there are stirrings up activity, with focus groups, Bible study, gift unwrapping, mission work. Let's capture a VISION for our future, by assessing what we now are doing and what we should he doing. God has plans for us!

Welcome Home

Sue VanDerzee

▲ ▲ ▲

THE SERVICES OF THE PAST WEEK at Middlefield Federated Church have been truly special. The thought that kept running through my head as I watched people wander around in awe was "In my Father's house are many mansions." That is indeed how the addition-renovation feels right now—like many mansions—and as the Sunday school rooms in the old fellowship hall are completed, the mansions will multiply.

As the new building begins to feel like home over the next weeks and months, the deacons will be studying and praying about how best to utilize this gift that we have helped to build for God. Surely, God wants this building to be here or the numerous objections and roadblocks faced along the way would not have been overcome. Surely, God wants us to continue and to grow the programs that nourish us and our children—Bible studies, worship, Sunday school, youth programs, women's programs, etc. But surely, also, God expects something more. What is that? Right now, we have no idea, but it is clear that with great blessings and considerable gifts come commensurate responsibilities.

We urge all of our friends and members to begin to think and to pray about this big question as we get used to and settle into the "mansion" with which we have been blessed. The answer will probably not come right away, and there's plenty of settling to do in any case, but considering the question is important. We are not given gifts and blessings so that we may "store them up in barns" but so that they might be of use in the world and advance the coming of God's kingdom on earth.

So, friends, welcome home and let the new works begin!

But How Do I Get There?

Roger Brewer

▲ ▲ ▲

FOR THE PAST TEN TO FOURTEEN YEARS, my wife Sharon has been having a particular recurring dream. It's sort of like a lost dream, but not exactly. The specific details of each dream are different, but the basic predicament in which she finds herself is always the same. She can see the place where she needs to be but cannot determine how to get there. She travels on various streets and roads, some familiar and some not so familiar, making turns here and there, struggling to find her way. She is confused and frustrated because in her searching she can still see her desired destination, but cannot find the road to take her there. In some dreams, she even loses her car.

Sharon and I have been trying to interpret this recurring dream for years. Yes, we believe dreams can be enlightening and/or instructive in our lives. Over the years, we've discussed various possible meanings of the dream but never arrived at an interpretation that was truly satisfying to us. Recently, as I was reading the Bible, I believe I finally got a breakthrough.

I was reading Jesus' teachings on why we should not worry about our lives (Matthew 6:25-34). In my mind, Jesus describes in this passage a place, not a physical place, but a mental, emotional and spiritual place where one can go and be without worry. What a beautiful place! Who in his or her right mind would not want to go there?

Throughout my life, I have read Jesus' teachings on worry over and over. I understand them. I believe in them. But I still worry about my life. I can see the place where I need to be but I cannot reach the destination. And I realize that this dilemma is not peculiar to worry, but pertains to other matters in my life as well. For example, I know I should not judge others but how do I get to that place mentally and emotionally where I'm totally free of judgment. I know I should love my enemy but how do I get to that place where I truly love even those who hate me. I know I should be at peace with myself though others may not be at peace with me, but how do I get to that coveted place of peace within?

For sure, the mere understanding of where you need to he does not necessarily get you there. What practices do you use to get mental, emotional and spiritual movement in your life? Do you use prayer? Do you turn to the sacraments? Does it help to talk it out with others? Do you use disciplines such as reading, meditation, or study? As far as I can tell there is no single formula. My guess is that different things work for different people, based on the circumstances and the points at which they find themselves in their journeys.

I am convinced that I get my most significant movement as a result of personal experiences. I certainly do not request these experiences. I wouldn't know what to request in the first place. I believe God Almighty brings certain experiences into our lives to help us grow. Many of these experiences are challenging. Some are painful. But we do get the growth.

Sharon's recurring dream has a lot of meaning for me. I can see the places where I need to go. I struggle to find the paths to get me there. I get impatient. I go up and down familiar and not so familiar streets. I make right turns, left turns and U-turns and occasionally I lose my car. I can still see the places. They seem to be right there in from of me, within arm's reach, but I just can't quite find the right path.

I pray and hope for the best for everyone on their individual spiritual journeys.

Always Accessible

Karen Bergenholtz

▲ ▲ ▲

ON MAY 1ST SEVEN OF US VENTURED TO NYC with other confirmation classes to learn of urban ministry projects. We encountered obstacles along the way, however, new possibilities and signs of faith presented themselves.

Physical accessibility at times was challenging: stairways, narrow doorways and curbs gave new understanding of travel by power wheelchair. We witnessed the steel beam cross at the World Trade Center site, a Burka-wearing woman, and Hassidic Jews leaving worship, wearing shawls and head covers.

Arriving at Anchor House in Brooklyn we celebrated the ministry of relieving addictions from men and women that had led to broken lives. Here we encountered accessibility—ramps, an elevator — and open hearts. The men and women shared song, skit and powerful testimony to the healing power of God. Relationship with God is key to recovery for them, as they report failed experiences of recovery in secular rehabilitation programs. Desperate for wholeness, Anchor House for many is a last resort. Allowing them accessibility to God makes the difference. We should all realize that God is always accessible to us, so why are we so determined to make it on our own?

Manifesting itself at Anchor House also is the feeling of sisterhood/brotherhood of "graduates" returning to support individuals still on the pathway. Accessibility showed itself again. As God empowers each person it is passed on.

I would venture a guess that those of us visiting Anchor House had never been in such state of despair as these residents. We were guests in their house, they were the welcoming hosts, and they ministered to us, reaching out to us however they could.

God loves us and wants us to keep Him in mind. What is it you need; what are you able to offer to God; what would God have you do in His name? Call Him anytime, He's accessible.

Faces of God

Sharon Roundtree-Brewer

O Lord, you God of vengeance, you God of vengeance, shine forth!
Rise up, O judge of the earth; give to the proud what they deserve!

(Ps. 94:1-2)(NRSV)

Come to me, all you that are weary and carrying heavy burdens, and
I will give you rest. Take my yoke upon you and learn from me; for I
am gentle and humble in heart, and you will find rest for your souls.

(Mt 11:28-29)(NRSV)

MY EARLIEST EXPERIENCES WITH RELIGION were through my grandmothers. It was my maternal grandmother who probably influenced me the most. I recall spending many summers sitting in her living room where she kept an enormous gold-labeled white book with beautiful colored illustrations. It was filled with bible stories and I spent hours sitting in that room reading those stories. Among others, I read about Jesus healing the sick, Jesus feeding the five thousand followers with five loaves and two fishes, and the joyous homecoming of the prodigal son. I was fascinated by all the stories I read and enthralled by the beautiful and detailed pictures. I'm sure I didn't understand all that I read, but in my childish mind all the stories seemed to be about loving, caring and accepting.

My most vivid religious memory involving my paternal grandmother occurred when I was probably no more then nine years old. I was sitting next to my grandmother in the back seat of the car and the family was listening to a sermon on the radio. I recall my grandmother listening to the sermon and shaking with fear. I also recall that I was more troubled by my grandmother's reaction to the preacher's words than the words themselves. She appeared frightened and her fear frightened me. Looking back I would now characterize the sermon we heard as a fire and brimstone sermon. The preacher was most likely talking about the strict requirements that God has for us, and what happens to people who don't obey those requirements.

I encounter many depictions of God as I read scripture—the strict demanding God, the loving caring God, and the vengeful judging God. I often struggle with some of these depictions. Recent news interviews with the authors of the books from the Left Behind Series seem to indicate that I might not be the only one wrestling with different interpretations of God and Jesus. In one interview the authors decry a view of Jesus that they characterize as wimpy.

As a little girl I embraced the loving and caring God that I had found when I read the bible stories in my maternal grandmother's living room, and I distanced myself from the vengeful and judging God that scared my paternal grandmother and me in the back seat of the car. Today, it is the love depicted by Jesus in Matthew 11:28-29 that comforts me and I still struggle to come to terms with the vengeful and judging God described in Psalm 94:1-2.

How many different faces of God have you encountered? Do you struggle with understanding any of them? I know that struggle is simply a part of my spiritual journey as I grow in my faith. Although I struggle, I continue to find strength and solace in God. May you always find the strength and solace you need in the Almighty.

Listen to God

Millie Simonzi

▲ ▲ ▲

LOVE AND LAUGHTER FILL THE newly painted rooms
  In every meeting, talk abounds concerning work to do.
  Still some things cause me to pause and think—
  There is plenty of time to complete the project,
  Even though we seem anxious to get it clone.
  Never forget, there is a bigger purpose for this building.

There is a beautiful sanctuary where you can sit and pray.
  Or maybe you choose the narthex to remember older times.

Get your spirit moving. What is God's purpose for the Middlefield Federated Church?
  Only if we search our hearts and minds will we decide.
  Do think about what you want this church to represent for the greater good for all.

LISTEN TO GOD! He speaks to each of us. What do you want this church to be for you? What is the vision you see for us in the future? What is the greater service we can do for the community, state and the world? The deacons have been spending a lot of time discussing this topic. Ponder these thoughts over the summer. Be prepared to step up and voice your thoughts. We all have a voice in determining the future for our church. We'll be calling on you!

God be with you.

Beginnings

Richard Kennedy

▲ ▲ ▲

WELCOME BACK! WE HAVE BEEN blessed with a beautiful summer and I hope it was a relaxing and rejuvenating summer for all!

As we enter the last quarter of 2004, we see numerous changes. We welcome our new organist and choir director who will lead our music ministry. We welcome you to our family! September 12 marks the beginning of our new children's ministry. My Faith Center is the exciting new curriculum for Sunday school that is interactive and will bring the stories and lessons of the Bible to life for our children. Youth fellowship will start the year off on September 19, bringing our older youth together for fun, learning and mission projects. Remember all are welcome from grades 7 to 12!

The deacons have a full slate, as we will continue to offer Faith Forums to discuss pertinent issues of the day as they relate to our faith. Needs the deacons have also chosen this time to embark on the Visioning process, which we feel will be an enriching and rewarding process for all members and friends of the Middlefield Federated Church. The goal of this process is to discover God's purpose for The Middlefield Federated Church and empower us to act upon it. To that end, all members and friends of our family will receive a personal invitation to participate in this very important process for the continued growth of our church family. In order for this endeavor to be a success, it is vital for all to participate. We need your thoughts, beliefs and most importantly your prayers. So come join us on October 17 at 11:30 a.m. as we explore what shapes our behaviors within and beyond the church. These are the choices we make that shape our lifestyles as individuals and as a congregation.

God's vision for the Middlefield Federated Church will be achieved with the help and faith of the entire congregational family.

God Bless.

We're Throwing a Values Party!

Sue VanDerzee

▲ ▲ ▲

PERHAPS YOU'VE HEARD OR READ about core values in District 13. The schools have been working hard with your children and/or grandchildren to encourage kindness, courage, responsibility, respect and honesty. Lofty goals, but they began with a party of sorts—a committee who thought about what were important values for life.

Our party at MFC is a little bit different. We're trying to discover, as the first part of a Visioning process, what makes our congregation special and unique. At the bottom of the question of who we are, are our values. What do we, as a group of Christian people, hold dear? What touchstones—or values—do we use to decide how we will act, where we will put our time, etc.?

Now that all seems perhaps a bit dry and serious for a party, but the deacons have worked hard to make this journey enjoyable. There are games and discussions and activities that will make our values as a group clearer, and we would like to share them with you on Sunday, October 17, at 11:30 A.M. That's after church, but come anyway even if you haven't made it to the worship service.

In the true spirit of celebration, there will be food and fellowship (and childcare for those who need it).

The journey will be much more meaningful if you take it with us. In fact, if it's not a congregational journey, with all of the congregation, it just won't be a fruitful journey at all. So, we're asking God's Spirit to accompany us and setting off to discover who we are and who God is calling us to be. Please join the party.

Gratitude

Beth O'Sullivan

AS I SIT DOWN TO WRITE this segment of the *Red Doors* I have several feelings and memories to express. Today as the leaves are falling all around my home it is a glorious warm fall day which is not always typical for the early weeks of November. Traditionally, I would just count the warmth up to the weather of the day yet, when writing I look up to God to see that this warm day is clearly a message and vision from him. A message to remind us that lie is always with us. Personally, I have had several of these messages this year but I feel our church has been blessed to have these messages too.

This time of year as, our fore fathers did, we start the holiday season being thankful with the celebration of Thanksgiving. We are thankful for food, safety, the comfort of home, family, friends, for the power of prayer, and God's steadfast grace. Yet, with thankfulness comes gratitude.

Gratitude rather than plain thankfulness has a more intensive demand. Gratitude has a depth of meaning which carries the feeling into action. Gratitude inspires us to do for others as they have done for us. We must minister and carry on as God has taught us through the teachings of Christ. We are all ministers and are capable of continuing God's message to others. We don't usually use the word gratitude when we speak of giving thanks, but through our acts to help others we are continuing to do so. It may be the simple hello, the call to a shut in, the simple question of how are you doing? All of these acts are showing gratefulness, allowing us to be ministers in God's name.

As a quote on gratitude by Thomas Merton, "To be grateful is to recognize the Love of God is in everything He has given us and He has given everything. Every breath we draw is a gift of his love, every moment of existence is a grace, for it brings with it immense graces from him, Gratitude therefore takes nothing for granted, is never unresponsive, is constantly awakening to new wonder and to praise of the goodness of God. For the grateful person knows that God is good, not by hearsay but by experience, and is what makes all the difference."

Perhaps as the church continues the Visioning process in small focus groups in individual homes we will be able to channel our thoughts of thankfulness which will help us share the action of gratitude.

Yours in Christ.

Advent

Dorothy Waller

ADVENT! WE'RE IN IT! A time of preparation, a time of expectation and anticipation. The choir sings "Are we ready for the babe of Bethlehem...?", the congregation sings "Come, thou long-expected Jesus." It's all so wonderful and exciting. But, it is also a time of frenzied activities—of decorating our homes, gift buying, parties, vacations, end-of-year business wrap-ups and budget demands, school plays, band concerts, dance recitals, Santa Claus, elves, Frosty, Rudolph, ho, ho, ho. We're like the man in the TV commercial who has overspent his limit and he says "Won't somebody please help me?" How did it all become so costly and frenetic? (Why, even in our hurry, we sometimes "X" out "Christ" in Christmas, and use "Xmas" instead.)

The greatest gift was given to the world over 2000 years ago by a loving God who expected nothing more from us than an acceptance of His gift and our thanks. How have we managed to muddy it all up with this pre-holiday madness. We're caught up in the whirlwind and we can't seem to break free. We read "Twas the night before Christmas..." to our children, but do we also read Luke's account of Jesus' birth to them? Do we help our children understand that the very word "Christmas" has "Christ" in it, and that Santa Claus is not the central figure of the season? Actually, to be perfectly honest, perhaps Santa Claus is the central figure to us as well. And we sit silently while any mention of God and Christ is ripped out of public vocabulary and settings. Let's not let it be ripped out of our family settings as well.

Let's take a moment to step back and focus on God's amazing gift to us, and that, because of this gift, we can understand more fully who God is. And the best gift of all—through Him we can have eternal life. Hallelujah, Hallelujah, Hallelujah!

2005

Appreciating the Ordinary

Sue VanDerzee

▲ ▲ ▲

ONE OF THE THINGS THAT always surprises me is how blessed it is to be healthy.

We all know that intellectually, of course. Health is one of the things we typically pray for, and indeed, the deacons helped the Pastor last Sunday with a healing prayer opportunity for members of the congregation. We also pray every Sunday—and hopefully on other days as well—for the persons we know to be ill and in need of health.

However, on a personal level, when we don't feel well, life just does not go as smoothly. Everything takes more energy. Tiny annoyances seem outrageously upsetting. Plans must be put on hold, which leads to extra planning woes. Food doesn't taste as good—or at all. We want to be alone.

Then, when we get healthy again, doesn't the world seem new? To swallow without pain is a blessing. To sleep without waking up hacking and coughing is sweet beyond belief. To regain your appetite is delicious. To meet a friend on the street does not bring an inward groan of "please-don't-notice-me-I-feel/look awful" but a spark of happiness as we stop and chat for a minute.

How quickly that blessed feeling fades, however. All too soon—usually less than 24 hours later—health is no longer a gift, but a right. We feel good again, and things get back to normal. Most of all, we begin to forget to say "thank you" for the gift of health.

A popular song line says "You don't know what you've got until you lose it," and that seems so true in the midst of our daily blessings. The millions of injured and displaced victims of the December 26 tsunami around the Indian Ocean bear witness to the stark fact that so little is necessary to be happy—family, friends, a roof over one's head, clean water and enough food. Ordinariness would be so blessed for these people.

So, let us resolve in this new year to appreciate what we have—our security, our friends and families, our church community and our health, whatever it might be—for in such ordinary things God shows his rich and boundless love for his children.

Reflections in February

Roger Brewer

IT'S ALL SO VERY INTERESTING TO ME, to say the least, that so many people in the world who believe in the same God and the same Jesus and read the same Bible have strongly-held different opinions and beliefs on political and social issues such as abortion, same-sex marriage, the death penalty, economic policies, when to go to war if at all, and the treatment of certain individuals and certain groups. I believe for the most part that these different opinions and beliefs are genuinely held by people of good will who are strongly committed to respect others, do what is right and abide by the requirements God has set for humankind. I have been reflecting recently on what lesson or lessons God would have me learn regarding the situation I have described and what, if anything, I should do. But am I making this situation more complicated than it really is? Is this simply a matter of me being right on the issues and everybody else who disagrees with me being wrong? Or am I wrong on all of the issues? That would be simple too. Perhaps I'm wrong on some issues and right on others. That would probably be a realistic way of looking at the situation but still short, in my opinion, of an overall per-spective that teaches in an enlightening way. I don't know at this point what God would teach me regarding different opinions and beliefs on the issues I mentioned, but certainly I will continue to hope with all my heart and soul for enlightenment in due time. Meanwhile, I feel there's important work that I can and must do right now.

Some beliefs held by certain individuals, groups and organizations are so repugnant to me that I would withdraw from or never become involved in the first instance with such individuals, groups or organizations. However, most opposing opinions and beliefs I encounter today do not move me to that extent, though the temptation is great on those issues where it appears to me others have compromised on the requirements of basic human dignity.

I believe I have the right to express my opinions with passion, if I choose to do so. I believe I have the right to act energetically on my underlying beliefs. However, I feel in every case that my conduct must be responsible, civil and considerate of others. I believe God calls me in general to think and behave with love and respect in my encounters with people who hold opinions and beliefs that differ from mine, even when the disagreement is on issues of great importance to me. I believe God calls me to withstand the temptation to succumb to discourteousness, hostility and intolerance.

Jesus teaches us to love our enemies (Luke 6:27). People who disagree with me are not my enemies; however, the same principle applies. God's command to me is that I love them. To me, this means I should treat them with dignity and respect, care about them, pray for them in earnest, not treat them with hostility, spend time with them and not withdraw from their presence.

Love of those who hold opinions that differ from mine is very important to me. I pray for myself and for others who may also struggle on this issue. I pray for guidance, strength, courage and insight. I pray for deliverance from any traps or misconceptions. I pray ultimately that we may all be united with God's love and that all boundaries that separate us one from another may be removed.

Playing It Safe

Karen Bergenholtz

Before I built a wall I 'd ask to know
What I was walling in or walling out...

ROBERT FROST

IN CONTEMPLATING THE LENTEN READINGS we have been hearing over the past few Wednesday evenings, it is difficult not to take them to heart, to perform some introspection of myself. By example, this past week's reflection on how many of us avoid contact with God, and "reject the gift of faith that God gives to us" brought me to thinking about the freedoms and deeper living I miss through lack of faith.

To begin with, I avoid venturing into water over my head, especially where natural bodies of water are concerned, i.e., oceans, rivers. I prefer to play it safe, collect shells, stare out at the ocean, and walk the shore. But playing it safe leaves me out of activities that the rest of my family embraces. Swim out to the raft — never. Being concerned with self-preservation I miss out on much. Fear of the unknown, of what could happen, takes hold. Little faith.

Is it human nature to cling to that which we are able to see, feel, hear, smell, and touch? These are the senses that are awakened every day with life experiences. Without much invitation we are exposed to sights, sounds, odors, and tactile stimulations requiring reaction. To understand beyond the visceral requires more. That's where faith comes in.

One never knows the wonders available to us if the waters are not entered into. The nourishment to my being that God offers sustains more than any earthly sustenance, and yet I turn to the familiar time and again. What freedoms do I miss? What do I wall out?

And yet, God offers hope through the Resurrection. The invitation is there.

John 14:6 Jesus answered, "I am the way and the truth and the life. No one comes to the Father except through me."

The Sacred in Everything

Sharon Roundtree-Brewer

*And the king will answer them, 'Truly I tell you, just as you did it to
one of the least of these who are members of my family, you did it to me.'*

Mt 25:40 (NRSV)

I AM HAVING A WONDERFUL TIME discussing spiritual issues with
K. S. as we go through the confirmation process together. It has been joyful,
uplifting and enlightening. Recently, I had the occasion to again read and
reflect upon Matthew 25:31-46 during a discussion with K.S. about ministry.
Our focus in this particular session was on service to others. In the verses we
read, Jesus tells about the final judgment and he was commending those who
had invited him as a stranger into their home, fed him when he was hungry,
gave him drink when he was thirsty, cared for him when he was sick, and visited him when he was in prison. Those he was commending were surprised by
Jesus' words because they did not remember doing the things to which Jesus
was referring. Jesus' reply was the verse quoted above. In serving others you
serve and honor God. Service to others is a good thing.

However, these verses speak to me about more than just service. These verses say to me that I should see the sacred in everyone I encounter and by exten-
sion I should see the sacred in everything I do. When Jesus said 'when you did
this to the least of these . . . you did it to me, that means to me that God is in
each and every one of us. Unfortunately, it's not always easy for me to see this.

I can easily see God in many people, especially in those who dedicate their lives to others and who sacrifice their lives for others. But it is more difficult for me to see the sacred in the drunken person sprawled out in the gutter or the addict asking for a handout. It has occurred to me that seeing the sacred in the hospital volunteer or the fireman and policeman makes it easy to look up to them. While not seeing the sacred in the drunk, the homeless, the addict, or the poor can make it easy to look down on them even as we serve them.

In my faith journey, I continue to strive to see the same sacred, the same presence of God in all people. I understand that the God that is in whomever we see as noble is the same God that is in all of us whatever our circumstance. It is when this understanding is written on my heart, when I can see the same presence of God in everyone, that I can truly serve the stranger, the poor, the hungry, the thirsty, the sick, and the imprisoned as my brothers and sisters. Though I fall short, I strive to serve them with the same reverence and awe with which I serve God.

I try to focus on the sacred in all I do, because every time I focus on the sacred in what I do and with whom I interact, I feel that I strengthen my relationship with God. May you continue to strengthen your relationship with God in everything that you do.

Glad to Be Born in the U.S.A.

Millie Simonzi

▲ ▲ ▲

I CAN'T SEEM TO GET IT OUT OF MY HEAD—that visit to Haiti.

I was the youngest of three children, raised in Middlefield, in a not so affluent family, but one where I never had to worry about my next meal or a bed to sleep in or getting help if I didn't feel well. My parents, the loving people they were took care of those needs and I never gave it much thought.

My first husband, Ron whom many of you knew, was from West Virginia. Visiting his home state was my first look at people living a different life than me. We visited his mother a couple oft times a year in War, West Virginia. This was in the early seventies when Black and White was still very separate, people we visited (family and friends) all had shotguns in their homes, and life was pretty rough. Homes were wallpapered with paper bags; bathrooms were still outside and a lot of folks still cooked on wood stoves in the kitchen. Head Start was a big upcoming program to help the children prior to entering public schools. Many of those kids had breakfast and lunch at the schools. The primary occupation was working in the coalmines. Not too pretty a sight to see those men at the end of a working day. I thought that was the poorest I had seen. Still I returned home to Middlefield and life resumed as usual in a comfortable style.

Ron passed away and my life was at a standstill. Steven, my son and I had love and plenty to live on, so we picked up the pieces and moved on. The church became a very important part of my life and God was surely with us during those difficult years. As the story goes, I met John and peace and stability returned to our life. (Well, not always, but most of the time).

Now 15 years later, all retired and looking for interesting and fulfilling things to do, I ventured off to Haiti. I can say that life shouldn't be easy just because I was lucky enough to be born in the United States. Nothing is easy in Haiti! I heard on the newscast in Florida that local children in the school system are being tested for TB. The results showed that of the 23 identified as carriers, 15 were originally from Haiti. That should be no surprise as the average person in Haiti only lives to about 50-55 mostly due to lack of medical care for the diseases they carry.

Why do I keep saying all this—because I want this church to care? Our district has adopted Haiti as the country to which we will dedicate our mission funds. We told you that we had begun building a medical clinic and hoped to raise additional funds to complete the building, and to staff and supply it when completed. I hope to return next year, as do others who went this year and maybe some of you also. I don't want to wait to the last minute to start raising money for this cause. Therefore, starting in a couple of weeks, I will be placing a basket in the narthex, one Sunday each month with the hope that you can each join in the effort to fund this building.

Another donation is not what anyone wants to hear, but this is truly a way to give a little to a people who are desperately in need. A small donation each month may make it easier for us to reach our goal.

JUNE 15

A Prayer of Thanks

Richard Kennedy

▲ ▲ ▲

HEAVENLY FATHER, I CANNOT REMEMBER the number of years you have blessed me with the honor of sharing the lives of the youth of our church. Nor can I remember all the names or the countless events we have shared but I thank you Lord for showering me with the unlimited blessings I have received on this journey.

I see them now as young adults and I am filled with a special love and pride for what they have accomplished. I thank them Lord, for allowing me to be part of their lives, and their parents for trusting me to assist in their spiritual growth.

We had fun. The games we played and invented! (Catch ball, because we couldn't seem to master volleyball!!) Whiffle ball in the C's backyard, H-O-R-S-E in church parking lot (I won), softball at Peckham, bowling all over the state. The events: Father's Day Breakfast, confirmation sleepovers, cooking dinner at the shelter in Middletown, canoeing (trying) down the Housatonic, crop walks, car washes, hay rides, the murder mystery, the Christmas pageants, the 8:30 music service, Sunday School classes, the conversations, the movie nights (never could do an all-nighter), Tanglewood, and every year attempting to master First Sundays before the end of the year!

I think of the children Lord, that have blessed me over the years; The B's, the C's (especially N.C., the first to ask me to be his mentor for confirmation) the D's, the K's, the S's, the C's, K. V., N. B., K. L. (the Little Angel), V. C., J. P., J., A., J., W. I can't name them all but you all know who you are.

Dear God, I thank you for the blessing of two young ladies that will always continue to be blessings in my life. One has no choice, my daughter Sara, who keeps me young and shows me you, Lord, are constantly working with and through our youth by sharing the contemporary spirituals with me. The message of our Lord is coming in loud and clear to and from our youth. Then there is my adopted daughter K., a blooming rose who has done more to enrich my faith than any person aside of my father.

I thank you Lord for these blessings. I thank the youth of MFC for being the vessel God has used to bestow these blessings on me. All glory and praise to God.

Amen.

JULY 1

Summer Reading
Betsy Bascom

▲ ▲ ▲

MY BROTHER AND I WERE DISCUSSING OUR FAITH LIVES one day. I was looking for a daily devotional and asked him what he used. What he told me was a surprise. He said that as a part of his morning devotions he reads a chapter of the Bible daily. He is now on his second time through. My husband reads the Bible daily, often before bed. He has for years. It seems to center him. My aunt Dorothy Waller is reading the Bible for the third time. What do they know that I don't! These special people have such a strong belief in God and Jesus Christ and are very comfortable in their belief. They talk openly and easily about it, sharing with others their faith. I envy their comfort. I feel like I'm missing out on something that they have found.

As I have gotten more involved in the church through committees and classes and have gotten to know more of our church family, I realize how much more others know about the Bible than I do. With this has come the realization that in order to truly grow as a Christian I need to move from being a passive participant in my faith life to an active one. It's time that I make a serious commitment to my life as a Christian on a daily basis, not just for an hour on Sunday mornings. Maybe then I will feel comfortable sharing what I believe with others.

As I look around the church, I am amazed at the myriad opportunities there are to expand one's spiritual life, including adult education classes, faith guides for My Faith Center, missions, and evangelism to name just a few. Christian Education is currently soliciting responses to a survey about day and evening programs beginning in the fall. Responses are already coming in. I plan on participating in some of these opportunities in the fall. Maybe some of them will appeal to you and your quest to learn more about your faith.

In the meantime, this summer I plan on starting what my husband, brother, and aunt are doing. I am going to begin at the beginning and read a chapter of the Bible everyday. I will read my new study Bible, a gift from my aunt, along with the notes, and learn. I am determined that this commitment will stay with me through the busyness of the rest of the year and that I will be able to complete my first reading of the Bible and begin on my second and then my third. If anyone reading this decides to make the same commitment, let me know. We can share our experience together!

Wishing you all a peaceful summer!

Disaster Meets Prayer Again

Beth O'Sullivan

▲ ▲ ▲

WE NEED YOUR PRAYERS AND HELP! I along with many of the congregation am constantly watching CNN, MSNBC, local and national news, and news specials all with concerns over the tragic events of hurricane Katrina. I must say it was on a Monday, the first day of school for me at Quinnipiac University that I began being mesmerized to the TV with concerns over the upcoming storm and it's aftermath; Hoping and praying that people would reach shelters and be safe within them. Oh what we all know now.

Yet, through the situation we pray and hope that all the individuals involved hear and feel God's presence. We pray for the frail, young, old, for the evacuees, and especially for the un-rescued. Give sustenance to those without food and water, give hope to the hopeless, give care to those who need medical attention and to little children who have lost the many items that give comfort and support in times of distress. We pray for strength and courage for the relief workers, first-responders police, fire officials, National Guard, Coast Guard, medical personnel and the volunteers who have come to assist. We pray for God's will to be done in all who are involved in this national tragedy, we pray for those who know Jesus and are encourage by his love and especially receive God's grace. We pray those for who may not know Jesus and ask them to trust in him. We pray for our church, and ask God to show us how we can send our angels to all that are in need.

But how do we help? How do we perform the great good so many miles away? In some ways it seems very difficult and in some ways it is very easy. We all can be involved — every little bit helps. Even in the midst of this profound tragedy Jesus' love and Gods light abound, God is working in our ability to help in the healing. We can go to our state and local collections agencies. Log on to the UMC or UCC denominational web sites for important information where donations can be given. Create health kits and school kits for all in need. Even the most simplest of life's conveniences we take for granted and are so needed, toothbrushes, toothpaste, baby wipes, diapers, a comfort item for children, food, can openers, hand sanitizer, deodorant, tee shirts, socks (babies through adults), blankets. Lend a hand for a few hours at a collection agency, or become part of the local mission team that can be called up in 24 hours notice for a disaster relief trip. The time is now but be prepared for continued help for a long period of time.

There is much work to be done in the gulf region and here at home within our own church. Help us serve our brothers and sisters affected by national disasters. Together we all can make it happen—Jesus and God are guiding us and blessing us along the way. Let us pray for all of those suffering trial and tribulation and help them to feel free to call on The Lord in the name of Jesus and be comforted by the Holy Spirit. Let them know that God said I will never leave you or forsake you. Psalms 22:19—"But thou, O Lord, be not far off! O thou my help, hasten to my aid!"

"Why Meets What:

A Congregational Call To Prayer"
Why another storm?
Why more devastation?
Why more human suffering?
Our whys go unanswered?
Until we determine what we
will do in the meantime.

Prayer moves us toward:
A compassionate "what"
That leads our hearts
And hand to God

When tragedy strikes.

Pray with groans
Pray in silence.

Pray with actions —
But by all means pray!

—From the Global Board of Discipline —

"Preparations"

Claire Piddock

*Do not boast about tomorrow, for you do
not know what a day may bring.*

PROV 27:1 (NRSV)

JUST THIS PAST WEEKEND, WE traveled to Maine to close up our cottages for the winter. The preparation includes putting away all outdoor equipment, disconnecting all appliances, covering the doors and windows with plastic, removing all perishable foods, sealing any staples that can survive the winter, and storing linens and paper goods in plastic containers so the critters who always seem to get in anyway will not shred them to make nests.

Like animals that grow thicker coats, store an extra layer of fat, bury nuts and seeds in the ground or stash them in tree hollows we are all making preparations for the cold of winter. Some of us, like many birds, even "fly" south too!

Part of this yearly ritual for me is sitting for some minutes in a location on a rocky pine-scented point above the lake, a place that always seems to calm my soul, a place where God seems especially close ~ and thank God for this haven of peace and serenity. This year, as l prayed my thanks, I thought about my faith as a preparation for life. Life comes at us fast, sometimes with happy surprises, good times, and unexpected pleasures, but also with sickness, loss, disappointments, and failure.

What can we do about this unknown future? We can walk with God, live in faith, and trust in Jesus. It is not always easy. I have to remind myself often to trust in God's plan for me. He knows the plan; I seek to understand it, and to live faithfully.

> *For you need endurance, so that when you have done the will of God,*
> *you may receive what is promised. For yet "in a very little while,*
> *the one who is coming will come and not delay; but my righteous*
> *one will live by faith. My soul takes no pleasure in anyone who*
> *shrinks back" But we are not among those who shrink back and*
> *so are lost, but among those who have faith and so are saved.*

HEB 10:36-38 (NRSV)

Illness may test our endurance; failures may test our flexibility, loss may test our creativity, but preparing our hearts for the love and grace of God will renew us, time and again, in any season.

What We Do Best

Sue VanDerzee

▲ ▲ ▲

ONE OF THE SURPRISING THINGS about my recent ten days in Biloxi, Mississippi with a group from Volunteers in Mission of the United Methodist Church was how very often we heard the beleaguered residents say, "thank you," and add, "If it wasn't for the people from the churches..."

Our experiences as we traveled about the city bore out this sentiment. On almost every street we worked, another church group—from Indiana or Tennessee or Arizona or Alabama—would be working also. They came from all denominations and from combinations of denominations—Catholics, Lutherans, Methodists, Baptists—covering the whole Christian spectrum. They were augmented by the large operations of the Salvation Army and the Red Cross, but basically it was people from churches all across the nation who were doing the scut work—in this case, cleaning out and gutting flood-ruined homes and getting to know the families who had lost so much.

Perhaps I shouldn't have been so surprised. Maybe such on-the-ground, getting- your-hands-dirty work fulfills some of the church's most significant commands—feed the hungry, clothe the naked, care for the widow and the orphan, proclaim good news to the poor. It made me truly proud to be part of such a group—in both the smaller and the larger senses—proud to be carrying on that work that Jesus' entrusted to his followers and humbled by the opportunity to serve people who had so much to teach even while they found themselves in such a desperate situation. Which brings me to what I learned in Biloxi. . .

Everything goes better with prayer—preferably before, during and after...
"It's all just stuff" as one woman, standing in the middle of her empty and gutted house, told us serenely... "Our real treasures are—or should be—in heaven," chimed in her neighbor, who at 78, was cleaning out his wrecked and flooded kitchen "so nobody else will have to smell it." . . . "We are blessed," a sentiment shared by everyone we worked with and for . . .

God will provide whatever we need in every circumstance. Just ask K. S. or me about the broken truck, the first Friday of work with no tools, the teddy bears, the answers to prayers, the indescribable feeling of resting in the arms of a loving God while trying to be his hands in a very needy place.

God's richest blessings to you all.

A Christmas Wish List

Roger Brewer

▲ ▲ ▲

THIS YEAR I'M MAKING A CHRISTMAS WISH LIST not of material things that 1 may desire, but of various no material items important to me. I am including general requests as well as requests of a very specific nature. One specific request I'm including pertains to the Deacon-sponsored Faith Forums currently being held at our Church. It is my hope that these Faith Forums continue into the future with greater participation from the congregation.

You may recall that we held our first Faith Forum on October 28, 2003. Thus far we've held a total of Fourteen Faith Forums on various topics of interest.

2003
October: Separation of Church and State
December: Euthanasia

2004
January: What is Your Idea of Heaven?
February: Faith and Politics
March: The Movie "The Passion of the Christ"
April: Homosexuality
May: War
June: Open Discussion
July: American Flag in the Sanctuary

2005
April: The Death Penalty
May: ls Jesus the Only Way?
June: Challenges Facing Prayer Today
October: Suffering
December: Holiday Feelings (Blue Christmas)

The purpose oft he Faith Forums is to provide an avenue to explore our beliefs and faith as they pertain to specific events and occurrences in the world. For example, although we may all believe, as Jesus taught, that we should love our neighbor, what does "love our neighbor" mean to each of us in times of war? There are often no simple answers and people hold different opinions on the topics we consider. We actively listen to one another and respect those who hold opinions that differ from our own. Indeed, the Faith Forum is not a place necessarily to come for answers, but a place to discuss how our own personal faiths lead to us to think and act about a particular issue. We believe that as a community of faith we strengthen and encourage each other by sharing our faith stories.

Also on my Christmas Wish List, I'm wishing everyone a true celebration of Christmas. May we all be especially aware during this holiday season of the presence and power of the Almighty God in our lives.

2006

Hold Fast

Karen Bergenholtz

A strong wind was blowing and the waters grew rough. When they had
rowed three or three and a half miles, they saw Jesus approaching the boat,
walking on the water; and they were terrified. But he said to them, "It
is I; don't be afraid." Then they were willing to take him into the boat,
and immediately the boat reached the shore where they were heading.

JN 6:18-21

I'M SURE MANY OF US KNOW THIS PASSAGE from the New
Testament, with the image of Jesus walking on water commonly recognized
by Christians and non-Christians alike.

Two other versions of this same event are also found in Matthew 14:22-33
and Mark 6:45-52. Looking at the passages in Matthew, we also see Peter leaving the boat to join Christ walking on water, but as Peter takes his focus off
Christ, and instead sees the power of the wind and waves, he begins to sink,
and cries out "Lord, save me!" Of course Jesus saves Peter.

Would you be more frightened of being tossed about by wind and waves or
by this vision of someone walking on water? It seems the disciples do not recognize Christ as the individual treading on water, and are frightened. Are we
more apt to fear what we recognize as an earthly threat, such as being battered
by wind/waves, or by the vision of something beyond our comprehension?

When the disciples recognize Christ they are "willing to take him into the boat." The question I ask myself is how many storms I worry through because I fail to recognize the power of Christ in my life.

When next you are in the sanctuary take a closer look at the stained glass window of Christ. The words are there above the figure of Christ for all to witness: "It is I, Be not afraid." May they be a reminder to hold fast to Christ through all kinds of weather.

In His Steps

Sharon Roundtree-Brewer

▲ ▲ ▲

A FEW MONTHS AGO THE PASTOR PREACHED A SERMON in which he mentioned a novel by Charles Sheldon called *In His Steps*. The Pastor explained that the acronym WWJD, which became very popular a few years ago and could be found on bumper stickers, jewelry, bookmarks and just about anything else, probably had its origin in Sheldon's book which was first published in 1897. The book was a compilation of a series of sermons that Sheldon had preached. In those sermons the members of a congregation were challenged to first ask the question "What would Jesus do?" before making any kind of moral decision in their lives. The Pastor put a little different twist on the phrase, asking instead "What would Jesus have me do?" (WWJHMD). The sermon and the Pastor's approach interested me so much that I borrowed the book to read. It made a strong impression on me, and since then I have read some other more contemporary nonfiction books with similar titles and themes.

Why did the book make such an impression on me? It's difficult to say. Depending on the situation or where we are in our faith journey, we all look at Jesus in different ways at different times in our lives. But as I think about it, I must say that Jesus as a moral example has always resonated with me and reading the book reinforced my sense of Jesus as an example and teacher in my life.

That being said, all questions that I face and all predicaments in which I might find myself are not always easily answered by asking the question

"What would Jesus do?" or "What would Jesus have me do?" For example, when I ask myself what would Jesus have me do in the area of helping the poor or loving my neighbor. The answer is clear. However, when it comes to some more controversial social issues facing the world today (some of which we've discussed in our faith forums), the answer to the question is not always as clear. Although the answer to the question is not always clear, in my view, we must continue to ask the question. Because every time I ask the question, "What would Jesus have me do?" it places my focus on Jesus. And it is always important and right to be focused on Jesus, especially during times of uncertainty. It is through him that we find our way.

> *"We do this by keeping our eyes on Jesus, on whom*
> *our faith depends from start to finish"*

HEB 12:2 (NLT)

Cleansing

Karen Bergenholtz

When you enter the land of Canaan, which I am giving you
as your possession, and I put a spreading mildew in a house in
that land, the owner of the house must go and tell the priest "I
have seen something that looks like mildew in my house."

LEV 14:33

MIDWEEK IN GULFPORT, MISSISSIPPI (IN the community of Turkey Creek to be exact), relaxing after dinner one night, I decided to thumb through my Bible. Amazingly enough, the Book fell open to Leviticus, with the caption "Cleansing from Mildew" staring up at me. How appropriate. Participating on the "demo" crew, our job was to gut a home to wood framing, scrub the 2x4s, bleach and rinse, bleach and rinse. At times the work was tedious and seemingly endless, compared to other job sites with our group where interaction with homeowners, or a sense of accomplishment through construction was possible.

So seeing the scripture passages explaining how to proceed with cleansing a house at least gave me a sense that my work was meaningful, at least important enough to be thoroughly dealt with in Leviticus. To step out on a limb, I'd say the procedure in Leviticus is more thorough than that laid out by FEMA in their brochure "Mold and Mildew, Cleaning Up Your Flood

Damaged Home." It even involves the priest purifying the house with two birds, cedar wood, scarlet yarn and hyssop. I will say no more, and am sure the Pastor would be grateful that we simply use chlorine bleach these days.

I spent a lot of time talking to God that week in Turkey Creek, trying to understand, trying to gain perspective with the devastation we were in the midst of, hoping somehow I was making a difference. God helped me carry many an armload or wheelbarrow full of debris.

Today as I write this, is Mardi Gras, Fat Tuesday, Shrove Tuesday, a day when cupboards are cleansed of "fat" in preparation for Lent and fasting; fill ourselves with calories now with the expectation that we cleanse ourselves throughout Lent.

The Gulf Coast will see a cleansing for years, physically, emotionally, spiritually. Having spent the week with a good deal of mold and mildew, I cannot help but examine myself for disease, and attempt to cleanse myself physically, emotionally, physically.

The people of Turkey Creek, Gulfport, and Biloxi I met are of strong faith and hope. Those qualities shine, and are of stronger contagion than the mold that permeates. It is the people that I remember, who inspire me to deepen my faith, to strengthen my relationship with God, to cleanse myself.

"The Faster I Go, the Behinder I Get"

Barbara Carlin

YOU KNOW THE OLD SAYING about "the faster I go, the behinder I get!" Seems like some weeks I just can't get caught up with all the little odd jobs, household tasks and work projects that I have set for myself or someone else has set for me. The "to-do" list just seems to get longer and longer. I've tried to rearrange, reschedule, eliminate and reorganize, but still the list goes on and on.

I'm not a particularly good house cleaner. Now, there is a difference between having a clean house and being a good house cleaner. I have a clean house; I'm just not a good house cleaner. What takes me 5 hours to clean might only take a good house cleaner an hour and a half. I find myself picking up something from one room, carrying it to another room only to find myself an hour later still carting that same item around. And eventually I realize all I had to do in the first place was to either throw the item away the first time I picked it up or finish one room before I move on to the next.

I sometimes have the same problem at work. I start one project only to be interrupted with a phone call, a billing error, a distraught patient or in some cases distraught employee. And the next thing you know: I'm "behinder."

All the efficiency experts will tell you that I need to learn to multi-task, reorganize, and prioritize. They may be right, but there is one thing they have forgotten to add to this list. Praying and prioritizing go together. And prayer should be at the top of the priority list. A little prayer goes a long way in helping us to refocus on our priorities whether at home, in the work place or anywhere we happen to be when we get that feeling of being overwhelmed by the "to-do" list. Whether a silent plea for help, a conversational request for assistance, or a loud scream for intervention; God hears them all.

> *Who of you by worrying can add a single hour to his life? Therefore,*
> *do not worry about tomorrow, for tomorrow will worry about itself.*

MT 6: 27, 34

What Brings Us Together?

Claire Piddock

▲ ▲ ▲

LOOK IN THE *RED DOORS*, usually on page 2 or 3. You'll see the Lectionary Readings. I wonder how many people actually read them or even notice that they are there. What is a lectionary? It is a series of Bible passages to be read throughout the year in a particular order. If we were to read, ponder, and discuss the same passages each week, what a blessing that would be! How it might bring us together to deepen our understanding and strengthen our common faith. Whether based on lectionary readings or not, any of our faith-based discussions serve the same purpose.

- The Pastor's sermons do. We can talk about the message and talk about our faith during fellowship, at committee meetings, or at Women's Christian Fellowship activities, men's breakfasts, or even during conversations of the Divine Secrets of the Dirty Diapers. The importance is that we talk about our faith.
- So do our Bible Studies and other adult enrichment opportunities. We are fortunate to have Bible studies in various formats, some pastor-led, and others led by us, taking turns with guidebooks that help with suggestions, readings and questions. The importance is that we talk about our faith.
- So do our Faith Forums with topics ranging from healing and prayer to abortion and the death penalty. And the new Faith Forum magazine is providing more opportunities for us to share our faith journeys

and talk about how our beliefs affect our everyday behavior. The importance is that we meet and share and by doing so strengthen the church body because we're talking about our faith.

* So do our multiple opportunities for service whether at the Durham Fair or in Biloxi, Haiti, Middletown, or Maine missions. They bring us together with others for faith in action according to our gifts and interests, and we talk, share, and develop more common bonds.

I imagine the church as a huge brain with the neurons (us) connecting in various and multiple ways, crisscrossing and intermingling to develop stronger connections—and consequently a stronger faith community.

Both Old Testament and New Testament readings preach the coming together of diverse peoples, using individual gifts and talents, to study, to talk, to act...to become one body, and one congregation dedicated to God.

> *"All the people gathered together in the square by the Water Gate. They told the scribe Ezra to bring the book of the law of Moses which the Lord had given to Israel. Accordingly, the priest Ezra brought the law before the assembly, both men and women and all we could hear with understanding . . . So they read from the book, from the law of God, with interpretation. They gave the sense, so that the people understood the reading."*

> NEHEMIAH 8: 1-2,8

> *"For just as the body is one and has many members, and all the members of the body, though many are one body, so it is with Christ. For in the one Spirit we are all baptized into one body—Jews or Greek slaves or free—and we are all made to drink of one Spirit. Indeed, the body does not consist of one member but many."*

> I COR 12:12-14

I urge you to try one of the multiple ways our church offers to strengthen our bonds and grow in faith. More than that, I challenge you to try something new for you, something that you did not do before. That's what brings us together.

What?

Roger Brewer

I'VE BEEN TOLD ONCE OR TWICE recently that I'm "hard of hearing." I have to admit that there have been those rare occasions when someone has said something to me and I've stood there without a clue of what he or she had just said. However, I deny being "hard of hearing." I can hear as well as many. It's just that on rare occasions what people say to me just doesn't register in my mind. Be patient, just give me a moment and everything will connect. If not, I'll just have to ask that the comment or question be repeated. The problem is not disinterest, hearing loss, or difficulty in understanding the language. The problem is that too often I find myself preoccupied thinking about people, things, and occurrences outside the moment at hand.

My mind takes me many places. How will I get up the leaves this fall? How about the snow this winter? What can we do to get people off illegal drugs? What can we do about poverty? Shouldn't I be doing something now to prepare for the next hurricane when it hits Connecticut? There must be an energy source for our homes and cars that we've never thought of. What can we do to tear down the barriers that divide us? You get the picture, don't you? And I'm not always thinking of the future. My mind also takes me to the past. I think about my mistakes and missed opportunities. I think of past achievements and good times.

I've got to find a way to stay home. But don't get me wrong. I don't believe we should always be focused exclusively on the moment. Indeed, we must think ahead and reflect on the past for our growth and prosperity, individually and as a society. Thinking ahead or reflecting on the past is not my problem. My problem is that I'm obsessive with it. I'm sacrificing too much of the moment in anticipation of a better day. What I need in my life is more balance.

In trying to get a spiritual perspective of my situation, I have been led to ponder a similar question of even greater importance. Am I too preoccupied with living life for the purpose of getting into heaven? If that is SO, am I missing opportunities of the moment to serve, to love, and to be loved? Does it matter to God if I love my neighbor because I want to go to heaven or love my neighbor because I love my neighbor, with the expectation of nothing in return?

I believe God would have me understand that there should be no conflict within me about today and tomorrow. During his ministry, the Pharisees asked Jesus when the kingdom of God was coming. Jesus answered, "The kingdom of God is not coming with things that can be observed; nor will they say, 'Look, here it is!' or 'There it is!' For, in fact, the kingdom of God is among you." Luke: 17:20-21. Can I interpret scripture to mean God's kingdom extends even to where I am at this very moment, if I'm open and ready to receive it? If it is so and if I can truly believe it, my anxiety about the future will certainly diminish.

I pray for myself. And if you too are struggling with balance in your life, I pray for you as well. May we all continue to celebrate God's presence in our lives in our blessings and in our struggles and in everything we do.

Tilling the Soil, Planting the Seeds, Waiting for Growth

Beth O'Sullivan

Jesus said, "A sower went out to sow. And as he sowed, some
seed fell on the path . . .. Other seed fell on rocky ground . . ..
Other seed fell into good soil and brought forth grain."

Mk 4:3-5,8 (NRSV)

PLANTING A GARDEN HAS BEEN one of my favorite hobbies and I frequently find myself in the throws of spring waiting and counting down the days to be in the garden. However, this year has been a challenge—the garden is in and the rain has come. Most recently I was at the garden store and purchased a packet of seeds. While in the checkout line the cashier asked, "Are you planting or replanting," my immediate answer was "re-planting".

Later in the day, while tending the garden, I realized that some plants that I originally thought were lost were growing and starting to bloom in the rich soil. Some seedlings were struggling in rocky ground; other plants were tangled in weeds. Seeing the result of my planting, I thought about Jesus, who like the sower in the parable, went daily lovingly and lavishly scattering words of grace. He was unconcerned if some words fell on rocky ground or in the weeds. Jesus willingly gave everyone the opportunity to listen and respond. He instinctively knew that some seed would fall on good soil.

Seeds represent the potential for growth and renewal that exists in every living thing. What we see in nature God calls us to see in ourselves. Seeds remind us of the human capacity to overcome obstacles, to learn, to heal, and to start over if necessary. Jesus tells us to place our faith in this capacity. This means we must trust it, we work at it, and we celebrate it everyday of our lives. We are beautiful and diverse as flowers, but we are much stronger. Inside each of us is the strong, tough little seed of faith, a faith that can handle anything.

We all must sow God's seeds. Plant some seeds of love intentionally today through the many small opportunities to say and do good deeds among your family, friends, acquaintances, and strangers. Ask God to guide you and help these seeds grow and produce more. Everyday words, dreams, acts of love and kindness have a way of growing far beyond what we can ever imagine, especially with God's help.

Salvation

Sharon Roundtree-Brewer

▲ ▲ ▲

AT OUR NEXT FAITH FORUM, we will be discussing opposing beliefs of salvation and grace: the belief that God's grace extends to everyone and therefore everyone will be saved versus the belief that God's grace is conditional and extends only to those who believe and behave according to God's requirements (only certain people will be saved).

In our discussion of the belief that God's grace extends to everyone, we will focus largely on the book *If Grace is True,* written by two pastors, Philip Gulley and James Mulholland. Gulley and Mulholland offer their controversial belief that eternal salvation is extended to everyone through God's perfect grace. The author Philip Gulley is a Quaker minister, writer, husband, and father. He has written other books and lives in Danville, Indiana. The author James Mulholland is a theologian with ecumenical experience in the American Baptist and United Methodist denominations. He is also the author of the book *Praying like Jesus* with which you may be familiar.

In our discussion of the belief that God's grace is conditional, we will focus in part on the points made by Dr. William Lane Craig in a debate called "The Craig-Bradley Debate: Can a Loving God Send People to Hell?" found on the internet. Craig is an American philosopher, theologian, New Testament historian, and Christian apologist. He is married and lives in Atlanta, Georgia, and is currently a Research Professor of Philosophy at Talbot School of Theology, Biola University in La Miranda, California. Contrary to the opinion offered by Universalists, Craig believes that a loving God can allow people to spend eternity in hell.

In addition to sites on the World Wide Web and other articles, we will also use John Sanders book, *No Other Name, An Investigation into the Destiny of the Unevangelized,* as a reference. Gabriel Fackre of Andover Newton Theological School has said, *"No Other Name* is the most comprehensive review available of historic and contemporary positions on the question of the ultimate destiny of those who do not hear the gospel in their lifetime."

I strongly recommend both books to you; however, you will not need to read them in order to come to the Faith Forum. We will provide you with enough information for you to fully participate in the discussion during the Faith Forum.

As you think of the two opposing beliefs on God's grace, you might find yourself strongly attached to one or the other and cannot envision that you would ever be convinced to change your point of view. So what would be the benefit, you might ask, in participating in a discussion on the matter? Some people may not be as confident on the subject as you are and may be able to grow from what you have to say. Additionally, although you may never adopt another point of view, you may be nourished or even caused to grow by questions and comments of others in the discussion.

Sheep and Goats

Karen Bergenholtz

▲ ▲ ▲

IF YOU HAVEN'T NOTICED, IT's fair season in the Northeast, with agricultural fairs displaying farm animals, and the labors of those who choose it as their livelihood. Without any true knowledgeable base, I wager fanning is a calling.

The barns on fairgrounds have always been a favorite diversion for me— my grandfather was a dairy fanner, and although his herd was sold off when I was very young, growing up next door, "the farm" as we called it, was my playground. Abandoned chicken coops were cleaned out and became a place to play house. Barn swallows nested abundantly, and always-wild kittens living in the grain room, "mousing" as their occupation, were culled to find the tamest, willing to be held. I would gather eggs from under nesting hens, with some making it harder than others, to slip my hand under their warm bodies and steal away those brown eggs.

Getting back to the fair, have you visited the goats and sheep? Baaa, naaa? I have to admit, I prefer the goats —they don't ignore you as the sheep tend to do. They're right up there, searching to nibble j anything.

So now read this:

> *"When the Son of Man comes in his glory, and all the angels with him,*
> *he will sit on his throne in heavenly glory. All the nations will be gathered*
> *before him, and he will separate the people one from another as a shepherd*
> *separates the sheep from the goats. He will put the sheep on his right and*

the goats on his left. Then the King will say to those on his right, "Come, you who are blessed by my Father; take your inheritance, the kingdom prepared for you since the creation of the world. For I was hungry and you gave me something to eat, I was thirsty and you gave me something to drink, I was a stranger and you invited me in. I needed clothes and you clothed me, I was sick and you looked after me, I was in prison and you came to visit me." Then the righteous will answer him, "Lord, when did we see you hungry and feed you, or thirsty and give you something to drink? When did you see a stranger and invite you in, or needing clothes and clothe you? When did we see you sick or in prison and you came to visit me." The King will reply, "I tell you the truth, whatever you did for one of the least of these brothers of mine, you did for me."

MT 25:31-40

My study bible explains that sheep and goats graze together, but are separated when it's time for shearing the sheep. Of course in Jesus' parable I would prefer to be considered one of the sheep. But maybe I really am a goat, herded off to the left. Usually the goats in the pen are interested in you as long as they think you have something to offer, and when you come up empty, they turn away, seeming as sort of "party animals", out for a good time. The sheep keep on nibbling away, nose to the grindstone, so to speak. So the question remains, who is more giving, sheep or goats?

In appreciation for all the sheep "whatever you did for the least of these brothers of mine, you did for me." And for the goats, for don't we make the sheep look that much better?!

I Needed a Plumber

Barb Carlin

There are different kinds of gifts, but the same spirit. There are different kinds of service, but the same Lord. There are different kinds of workings, but the same God works all of them in all men.

1 COR 12:4-6

I REALLY LOVE MY HUSBAND. I must! We've been married for 39 years. But—he doesn't know the business end of a hammer from a stump. And that's O.K. God has blessed him with many, many other wonderful attributes. And anyone who knows him will tell you he is a wonderful, loving, caring, spiritual, humorous individual. He has been a great father, a great husband and my best friend. What a Guy! But I needed a plumber! You know that sick feeling you get when you open the door to get something out from under the sink only to see water sitting in a puddle and a strange odor creeping up to your nostrils. In my case, I actually did notice the slightest of odors a few days prior, but chose to ignore it, thinking it was probably nothing, or at the very the least the garbage that had been in there for a day (or maybe two, or maybe three).

Nope! I needed a plumber. Once I got the courage to take a look under there and assess the problem, I knew immediately that I was out of my league. And as for Bob, he was gagging just thinking about carrying that sopping wet mess down to the garbage. Do you know how hard it is to get a plumber to take care of what turned out to be just a minor little adjustment? I really didn't care how much it was going to cost me (within reason). All I knew was that I had a problem for which I had neither the knowledge to fix, nor the tools. I threw a dart at the yellow pages under plumbers and hoped I would get one that would come within a reasonable amount of time and not demand my first born in payment.

I continued to think about this whole predicament for several weeks after. I had managed to get a good fellow who did a fine job and did not make me remortgage the house, but the whole scenario has remained in my mind for months. I could easily be in the same situation if I needed an electrician, a carpenter or any other skilled person for a minor job.

God really does spread the talent around. And as a church family, it would be nice to know what each of our gifts is. It would be reassuring to know who we could go to for help at specific times of need. Rather than throwing a dart at the yellow pages, I would like to know if there is someone within my church family that I could call on. Not only does God spread the talent around, but He also expects that we share that gift. In the coming months, I would like everyone to think about what they might be able to share. I am going to be revisiting this again when our mission team returns from Biloxi.

In the interim, think about the gifts that God has given you. Everything that God has enabled us to do is a gift in some form or other. Share the Gift.

You Can Never Have Too Many Flashlights

Claire Piddock

⩓ ⩓ ⩓

A FEW WEEKS AGO, THE Pastor began the children's sermon by asking what a flashlight was for. The question triggered a silent chuckle from me because of a hang-up I seem to have about flashlights. I never seem to have a working flashlight when I need one. I never have enough flashlights! It became a family joke. So, two Christmases ago, my daughter presented me with 12 different flashlights—all of different sizes and types. It was the best gift ever.

After all, we all need light to see in the dark, to find things, to find our way. But this need for light stems from a deeper human need for me and for all of us. Just think about light and ideas associated with light: radiance, brightness, sun, warmth, hope, joy, heaven. Meditating on light brings to mind, of course, Christ, the Light of the world who shows the way, who IS the way.

I am the Light of the world; he who follows me will not walk in the darkness, but will have the Light of life.

JN 8:12

So in this Advent season, bear with me as I do some free-associating with the word *light* and, without too much of a stretch, come up with the concepts of hope-peace-joy-love that we think about in Advent. I think of the *light at the end* of *the tunnel* signifying hope for the future-hope for the heavenly kingdom. I think *thy kingdom come* and *come all ye faithful*—prayer and the Christmas carol anticipating and linking, not only the birth of the baby Jesus, but the everlasting life that was the miracle of the resurrection.

I think of other carols and the words *peace on earth* and *sleep in heavenly peace*. The hope of the world lies in that peaceful little babe—Christ the Light. Following the Light as did the shepherds and Kings is the means for finding that peace on earth.

Lightness of spirit, that which makes you feel so light on your feet, you can jump up and dance, makes me think of joy—jumping for joy and *joy to the world* and *joyful, joyful, we adore thee*. And adoration implies love, the love for the babe in the manger, the love for God, and God's eternal love for us.

On second thought, the best gift was not the flashlights; it is and always will be God's gift of his son Jesus Christ. Amen.

2007

▲ ▲ ▲

Other People's Faith

Barb Carlin

But some will say, "You have faith, and I have works." Show me your
faith without your work: and I will show you my faith by my works.

JAS 2:18

AT A LAY SPEAKERS COURSE we were each asked to give a 3-minute message on "How has your faith in Jesus Christ changed your life?" I have always felt I had a fairly strong faith, but I never stopped to think about how it has changed my life.

I can't remember when I didn't have a faith in Jesus. I suppose when I was younger, maybe I didn't really know what faith was. I just know we always went to church on Sunday, attended all the church dinners, participated in our Youth Fellowship and said our prayers before bed every night. This was the faith I knew as a child and as a young adult. As I look back on my life, God has always been there, guiding me—even when I didn't want to be guided. H-m-m-m! Those must have been my teenage years. During those years He wasn't so much guiding me as He was protecting me from myself. I do know I thought about God in terms of always being with me and this was my perception of "faith".

My faith in Jesus began changing me only after I had my own family and was able to reflect on the importance of God in my life and the day-to-day caring for my family. Getting older probably had something to do with it too.

But the real truth of the matter is, my life and my faith really didn't change all that much until a year ago. That was when we went to Biloxi for the 1st time. *My faith in Jesus Christ didn't change my life; other peoples' faith in Jesus changed my life!*

Last week at this time I was in Biloxi, Mississippi with my husband and several other faith-based volunteers from our church and the UMC conference. If you want to see a testament to Jesus Christ and the personal faith that is built from a belief in our Savior, just take a trip south to Biloxi, Haiti, the Dominican Republic, or other areas ravaged by nature, war-torn strife or poverty. For those of you who have been to these areas, I'm preaching to the choir.

You can look at all the pictures the media can flash across the TV; you can read every article in Time and Newsweek; and you can let your imagination run wild, but you will never understand the complete and utter devastation hurricane Katrina had on the Gulf Coast and its people unless you see it firsthand, And by the same token you will never be able to believe the strength and faith the people living in this area have that has enabled them to survive, persevere, rebuild and continue their lives. To work with these people who have not only lost members of their families but neighbors and friends and in some cases every earthly possession they owned has renewed my faith in God, renewed my faith in the human element and renewed my faith in my own capabilities. You have not seen faith until you have met these people. They have not given up, they have not wavered in their commitment to their community, their neighbors, their church or to their great and awesome God. Even after almost a year and a half they are still fighting a battle to recoup their homes, their livelihoods, and their self-worth. And they are doing it through hard work, determination, and an incredible faith in Jesus Christ: a belief that God will lift them up and carry them through this hardship and on to a better life both here and in God's great heaven.

Rick Warren, in his book *The Purposed Driven Life*, has you spend 40 days in search of God's purpose for you in your life by contemplation and reflection. Spend a couple of days in any coastal town in Mississippi or the mountains of Haiti or the hills of the Dominican Republic and I can assure you, you can find a purpose without reading a book on it.

The faith of the people in Biloxi, Mississippi changed my life. They changed my definition of faith, they changed my faith in Jesus Christ, and they changed how I will live my faith from this point on. I challenge everyone to examine your own faith. The faith of the people of the on the Gulf Coast, Haiti, the Dominican Republic, and so many other places in this world are challenged every single day of their lives. Hold them in your prayers every day, and consider a life of faith through service. Faith is as much about our doing, giving, loving, caring, and helping as it is about God just being a presence in our everyday lives. Faith is in our every day lives.

Living Faith

Michael Waller

▲ ▲ ▲

WRITING A SHORT MESSAGE for the *Red Doors* does not come easily. So I greatly appreciate the thoughtful pieces from the Pastor and from fellow members of our church family which appear regularly in this letter. What to say, and how to say it?

After procrastinating for weeks, and wondering whether some great inspiration would hit me like a summer thunderclap. It did not, so I accept that I can no longer avoid what I agreed to do.

Ahh . . .that's it! Share my faith! But what is it? Well, I have faith that the sun will come up each morning that it will also rain sometime, that the daffodils and fruit tree blossoms will appear each spring. This knowledge is based on experience. It's always been this way, and so it will continue. We accept on faith that God created heaven and earth from a great void. Ever since God put the universe in motion we I mow that for everything there is a season, and we accept it and live with it in joy, and in times of trouble. Then there is faith in friendship, based on trust, and respect and openness. When I share something with you – a thought or something of material value I have faith that you will respect the sharing. In this we have earned one another's trust. But once again this is based on experience.

Faith is more than experience, and that is what I wrestle with. Faith is having confidence in what I cannot see, or am too weak to accept. Jesus faced such weakness many times among his disciples - Peter started to walk across the water but then sank; Thomas doubted. And isn't that my problem too? It is, but I can take hope in learning, as the letter to Hebrews says: faith is being sure of what we hope for and certain of what we do not see. Our Pastor stated it pretty simply a few weeks ago when he said that "faith is one step beyond logic". We know from our Old Testament that with faith Noah built the ark; Abraham stood ready to sacrifice his son, Moses led his people to the Promised Land. But even with faith there can be, and is, disappointment and suffering. Job was tormented but held fast to his faith; the prophets were scorned; Peter and Paul were tortured and killed for their faith.

We sing hymns like "Faith of Our Fathers, and "Great is Thy Faithfulness". We talk about being on a "faith journey", and indeed we are. On my own journey, I need the reassurance that Faith (with a capital F) is not something that can be striven for, but is something I must accept and rest in. And I find my faith renewed when I am still - frequently at night - and I sense the strength of "keep the faith . . . all is well". I know God sent His Son to save you and me and all who will claim him. My faith is a gift from God, and what a great gift!

Entering into Silence

Beth O'Sullivan

"As a deer longs for flowing streams, so my soul longs for you, O God."

Ps 42: 1

IN THE EARLY MORNING HOURS it is — dark, quiet, a time for reflection. Yet, my mind can quickly switch to the tasks of the day, at home and at work, switch into "Mom" mode. Have you ever tried to spend time in quiet — but listening to the voice that dwells deep in you heart? That quiet time when there is no radio to listen to, no TV to watch, no book to read, no person to talk to, no project to finish, no phone call to make. I found this made me realize how quiet I haven't been.

It is not always easy to enter into this silence and not listen to the loud sounds of the world. With this season of Lent and the time for sacrifice devotional prayer and Lenten readings have been added and changed my morning routine. However, in that moment of silence I am able to feel one step closer to God. I have accepted that there are issues that I need God's guidance and hand to watch over me. I have also had the pleasure of feeling a sense of renewal a sense of calmness to start off my day and know that the Lord is watching over me daily.

Our Pastor has preached about silence and offered us the challenge to make a sacrifice to spend time and commitment to God. Take time to create this spiritual atmosphere for yourself, thank God in the fact that he has blessed us with a very spiritual church. Find a devotional partner, come to Lenten soup and service, come to Bible study, visit churches, listen to spiritual music, and be with people who support your devotional time and spiritual commitment.

Take time to add silence into your life and be in prayer with God. To pray is to listen attentively to God. "When we dare to trust that we are never alone but that God is always with us, always cares for us, and always speaks to us, then we can gradually detach ourselves from the voices that make us guilty or anxious and thus allow ourselves to dwell in the present moment" (Henri J.M. Nouwen).

Pray with Us

Roger Brewer

▲ ▲ ▲

I ASK THAT YOU PAY SPECIAL attention to the notice "Invitation to Prayer and Meditation" that is included in this issue of the *Red Doors*. You are invited m make a two-week commitment (from April 23 to May 7) to sit daily in meditation and prayer in partnership with the Deacons. After the first two-week prayer/meditation session ends, there will be other two-week sessions at various intervals indefinitely into the future. The deacons will continue to invite the congregation to participate.

If you have not guessed it already, the idea to do two—week prayer/meditation sessions, and to invite the entire congregation to participate, was inspired by the practice during Lent when each Deacon partnered with another Deacon to meditate, reflect, and pray, including praying for each other.

Praying daily during Lent in partnership with another deacon was a very meaningful experience for me, with some very significant benefits. One special benefit was that it helped me to get back to praying on a daily basis.

I know, I know, I should have been praying on a daily basis already. I had been telling myself for quite a while that I needed to get back to prayer as I had known it in the past. I kept reminding myself, but for one reason or another, I never did it.

Now, don't get me wrong. It's not that I had stopped praying. It was nothing like that at all. It is fair to say that l was praying on a very regular basis However, I was not praying every day as l did when I was a young boy growing up in rural Georgia or as I did as a younger man struggling with my early ambitions.

In years past my prayers were not only daily, I feel they were much more intimate as I conversed with God. Additionally, I did not focus in the past primarily on asking God for things I want, as I'm inclined to do today. Instead, I focused in the past on understanding the developments in my life and my thoughts and feelings as they lit or did not fit with God's expectations and support of me in my journey.

How great it would be to get back to those days of daily prayer, when my praying opens me completely, and purges me of all clutter, leaving nothing, absolutely nothing, between my Almighty God and me. I am not at that place where I want to be, not yet, but certainly, I am moving in that direction.

My commitment during Lent to another deacon, and indeed to all of the deacons, to sit daily in meditation and prayer helped me with the discipline I needed to move closer to God. I was able to set aside time each day to meditate and pray because I had made a commitment to my fellow deacons, and I would do nothing, if possible, to dishonor that commitment.

Without question, it should not have taken a partnership to move me in the right direction, and perhaps in time, I would have been able to move in the right direction on my own.

However, I appreciate the reality that the partnership did in fact help me with my discipline, and for this gift, I am grateful.

Right now, I'm feeling that there must be a benefit or two for you if you partnered with others in prayer and meditation I hope you sincerely consider our invitation and ultimately join us in praying together, and for one another.

Musings

Karen Bergenholtz

▲ ▲ ▲

MOST OF US RECOGNIZE in receiving a *Red Doors* dated mid-month that it is a deacon's, not the Pastor's writing on the cover, with each assigned a certain month, scheduled far in advance. So I've known for months that May is my responsibility. Often, inspiration comes far ahead, and I formulate in my head what's on my mind, intending to put it to paper when the time comes. But every day is new, different and news of the world impacts daily. Weeks ago Mr. Imus was the news of the day, usurped by the awful tragedy at Virginia Tech.

At a special Faith Forum held to discuss the question, "Was God there?" agreement was "Yes", and it was not God's Will as some might question. We discussed how Cho Seung-Hui slipped through the cracks even with attempts at intervention, and what we can do if we recognize or suspect similar troubled individuals in our community. Our Pastor encouraged reaching out as Christ would have, to those who live on the edge of community. Thanks be for Elisabeth Kennedy who talked with children that day of what they might do when noticing a sad, lonely child at recess.

Months ago my instinct was to write about hospitality, as the deacons discussed this topic at our devotional meeting, and it remains pertinent, recalling how Christ receives the unwelcomed of society. Not all of us feel equipped to act as Christ, and comfort levels differ. Pete and Edna H. had no idea who Paul and I were in 1981 when we moved to Middlefield, but a simple hello at Fellowship Hour opened the door to this community of Faith. Feelings of inadequacy with Biblical literacy led me to participate in the Disciple class, with the result of being touched by God's word in my heart. How many of us feel ineloquent, unable to share what we know? But is it is hard? Do you believe that God loves you, and your fellow human beings? Is it difficult to simply let someone know that they are not alone, that we are not alone?

This morning it is raining outside, but I sit listening to the joyful galloping footsteps of our young cat Dolly running in the hall above my head. I can choose to see rain now, or look for sunshine later. Take strength in Paul's letter to the Philippians:

> *"Rejoice in the Lord always; again I will say, Rejoice. Let your gentleness be known to everyone. The Lord is near. Do not worry about anything, but in everything by prayer and supplication with thanksgiving let your requests be made known to God. And the peace of God, which surpasses all understanding, will guard your hearts and your minds in Christ Jesus.*
>
> *Finally, beloved, whatever is true, whatever is honorable, whatever is just, whatever is pure, whatever is pleasing, whatever is commendable, if there is any excellence and if there is anything worthy of praise, think about these things. Keep on doing the things that you have learned and received and heard and seen in me, and the God of peace will be with you."*

PHIL 4:4-9

We sometimes feel we have but a small voice, but consider this passage, take strength and courage, and "keep on *doing* the things that you have learned" with the knowledge that "the God of peace will be with you."

More Than Hospitality

Sharon Roundtree-Brewer

▲ ▲ ▲

MAY 27 WAS CONFIRMATION SUNDAY at the Middlefield Federated Church, and for me it was a meaningful and moving ceremony. The brief thoughts the mentors shared with us about the young person they had mentored for the last six months gave me a small glimpse into the personality and spirituality of these young people. The statement each confirmand made about what the Middlefield Federated Church meant to them was also enlightening. I felt privileged as a member of the congregation to share this part of the faith journey of so many of our young people at the church. In speaking with some of the parents of the newly confirmed members and other members of the congregation, it was apparent that the ceremony was meaningful and moving to them as well.

I found it interesting that so many of these young people said that one of the things they liked the most about the Middlefield Federated Church was that the church was so welcoming and that there was a very real sense of family within the congregation. As one confirmand expressed it, "We take care of each other." I have often heard other members of the congregation make this same point. In addition, on many occasions, I have heard participants of new members classes echo these same sentiments. And, as I think back to my initial experience with the church before I became a member more than twenty years ago, I must say that that was my experience also.

Scripture compels us to extend hospitality to strangers (Romans 9:13), and if what so many are saying is true, it appears that we as a congregation are doing a good job in this respect. However, I don't think that we should rest on our laurels. There must have been times when some people have not felt as welcomed as others. There must have been times that we neglected to open our arms. There must have been times when a stranger entered our midst and we overlooked them. Perhaps we did not recognize them as a stranger. Perhaps they gave off "do not approach me" signals. Perhaps that day we were too pre-occupied with our own problems to notice anyone else. Perhaps we just didn't recognize the loneliness in their eyes.

I have a prayer for our congregation. My prayer is that we always extend more than hospitality. My prayer is that everyone who enters our doors to worship with us feels welcomed. My prayer is that no one ever feels like a stranger in our midst. My prayer is that everyone who enters our church to worship with us feels as if he or she is a part of a family. May everyone who walks into our congregation to worship with us feel the care and love our confirmands feel.

Praise the Lord!
Richard Kennedy

ON JUNE 3RD THE PASTOR preached a sermon about the Trinity, (the Father, Son and Holy Ghost (Spirit)). At the time I was preparing this article for the *Red Doors* and having difficulty as the subject I wanted to address was singing praise to God. However something was missing. I could not express the importance of singing Praises to God aside from the utter joy we get from this form of worship.

You see I had forgotten what the result of singing praises to God is. There is a song named "When Praises Go up" and in it is says: "When praises go up God's blessing come down" and that blessing is the welcoming of the Holy Spirit into our presence.

How many times have you been going about your daily life listening to the radio, elevator music, or TV and heard a piece of music that grabbed hold of you and took you out at this world into a totally beautiful place? Disregard what kind of music it was. It could have been Pop, Jazz, classic, gospel, country, blues, bluegrass, even Rap. (Although I must confess I haven't heard one yet, but I'm sure after reading this my daughter or a member of my Sunday school class will present one to me!) For me one of the most spiritual pieces of music is Tchaikovsky's Piano Concerto No. 1 in B-minor. To me it shows how God blessed this man through the Holy Spirit to give mankind this wonderful gift. Others include: The Moody Blues " Greatest Hits", Gladys Knight's

"I feel a Song In My Heart" and "Storms of Troubled Times", any version of "Amazing Grace," and my personal best "His Eye is on a Sparrow".

In church we have certain hymns that I feel move the entire congregation and I begin to feel the entrance of the Holy Spirit — but we always stop at the end of the hymn! Which is just too soon to allow the Spirit to enter. Just imagine if we allowed ourselves the blessing of singing praises until we came to our and, until the Holy Spirit overflowed in each of the building and us and lingered with us through the rest of the Service. Wouldn't that be a wonderful experience?

Isaiah 38:18-20 says it best:

*For the grave cannot praise thee, death can **not** celebrate thee: they that go down into the pit cannot hope for thy truth. The living, the living, he shall praise thee, as I **do** this day: the father to the children shall make known thy truth. The Lord **was** ready to save me: therefore we will sing my songs to the stringed instruments all the days of our life in the house of the Lord.*

The dead sing the hymns with head down looking at the words, worrying about singing in tune and not loud enough to be heard by the person next to them never mind God.

We are the living, the living are filled with the Holy Spirit. Sing it loud and proud that you are praising God. We WILL be in tune and the Harmony will be a joyful noise unto the Lord. Shall we sing Praise to the Lord?

Amazing Freedom

Barb Carlin

Now the Lord is the Spirit, and where the Spirit
of the Lord is, there is freedom.

2 COR 3:17

I'M FEELING A TAD GUILTY. The Sunday before the 4th of July, one of our three deacon teams, minus me, presented the morning worship service which was centered around the theme "Freedom." I know how much preparation all of our deacons put into their programs and the nerves and stress that go along with getting up before a large audience. Even as forgiving a crowd as our congregation is, it is still a very intense 60 plus minutes. Thanks to you all. I owe you one!

Interestingly enough, the last weekend in July, Millie Simonzi and I traveled to Boston to attend the Women of Faith Conference and to my surprise and delight the theme for this year's presentation was "Amazing Freedom".

Prior to the conference, I guess my idea of freedom centered mostly around the freedoms granted me through our Constitution and Bill of Rights. But guess what? God through His Son Jesus Christ has given us more freedom than I could ever have imagined. We are not truly free until we accept the presence of God in our lives and the liberation from sin by accepting Christ as our savior.

How about a little freedom from worry! Read Matthew 6:25-34. Next time you find yourself worrying about something, whether it is a little or a large situation, give it up to God and free yourself from an outcome that you probably have no control over anyway. God is the one in control.

How about freedom from fear? Were you ever afraid that someone would ask you a question about the bible or your faith and you weren't sure that you could respond with an appropriate message? Read Matthew 10:19-20. God will give you the both the music and the lyrics.

There are times when fear goes a lot deeper than just verbalizing our faith. Some have the fear of heights, some the fear of water, and others the fear of crowds. God wants us to trust Him with all our fears and to reach out to Him for a secure and helping hand; the helping hand of love and freedom. Ask God to free you from whatever your fear is. Trust Him and earnestly pray for His guidance and you will truly be set free.

Truth

Michael Waller

BUT ABOVE ALL THINGS
TRUTH BEARETH AWAY THE VICTORY

THERE IT WAS. IT WAS painted in large maroon letters on a light colored wall behind the stage and lectern in our schools assembly hall which also doubled as a dining hall. You couldn't miss it, at least once or twice a day. It was at the school I attended from the sixth grade through graduation—so over a six-year stretch it was burned into my brain—and my classmate's brains—for more than six decades now. It's good advice, especially for young people, for oldsters, too. It pulls no punches:

> Tell the truth...victory. But also
> Avoid the truth, or lie.... defeat.

But what has this to do with our faith as Christians? Just about everything. Christ said in response to Thomas the doubters question (John 14:6) of how do we know the way to life eternal..."I am the way and the truth and the life - and no one comes to the Father but through me." What we know of Thomas is that he remained a faithful follower of Jesus although his doubts continued. Even after Jesus' resurrection Thomas needed to touch His wounds before he could exclaim "my Lord and my God." Jesus responded, "Blessed are they who do not see and yet believed".

Jesus asked to Peter, James and John before they went to the mountain with him... "who do you say I am?"... And Peter said, "You are the Christ (the Messiah) of God." Jesus affirmed many times that he was - and is - the Son of God. The Samaritan woman at the well said she knew the Messiah would come, and Jesus said simply "I who speak to you am he." Again, He said to the scribes who were baiting Him... "Before Abraham was I AM!" (John 8:58) And still later when He had raised Lazarus from death (John 11:25-26) "I am the resurrection and the life."

These are monumental declarations by Jesus and his disciples, and there are some sixty or seventy such claims in the four Gospels. Now, when Jesus made these claims, was he speaking truly? For me he was, and still is, and he asks us and invites us time and time again to accept what He says and does as true. I do, and I am frequently reminded of what I saw so many times as a boy —that truth beareth away the victory.

Cranberry Sauce, Squash, and Good Old Pumpkin Pie

Beth O'Sullivan

▲ ▲ ▲

A TYPICAL THANKSGIVING AT OUR HOUSE: turkeys, cornucopias, chocolate chip crescent rolls, two tables of people, and pilgrim hats. Hot stuffing from the oven, creamed onions, cranberry sauce and pumpkin pie. Aunts, Uncles, cousins to play with, Grandmothers, Grandfathers and family gathered around the table or the television watching football. Or the notorious family football game and after dinner walk. This is the typical vision of our family's thanksgiving.

But Thanksgiving? How much do our celebrations have to do with giving thanks? If one thinks of the first Thanksgiving one realizes the importance of thanking God. In December of 1620 when the Pilgrims landed on Plymouth Rock one clearly needs to give thanks to God. Through the dead of winter the pilgrims struggled with meager portions of food, strenuous tasks of building shelter, biting wind, cold and incurable diseases and death.

Yet, through out this trouble God sent messengers and protectors. God sent the Indians— Samoset, Squanto to help the settlers learn how to hunt, fish and plant crops that would flourish. With the bountiful harvest both the pilgrims and Indians gathered at the table to be thankful for God's goodness.

The pilgrims worked and toiled with the soil day in and day out to know how dependent they were on God's bounty. They learned to thank God despite the bitterness of the winters past. And they would thank God with his abundance of blessing too.

We teach our children to say "please" and "thank you" as a foundation of courtesy, yet it is so easy to forget to gratefully acknowledge God's blessing and goodness in our lives. A family tradition that is shared at our Thanksgiving table is to have each individual make a statement about what you are thankful for on Thanksgiving Day. May everyone lift up our praises to God on Thanksgiving and every day.

This thanksgiving let your prayers be lifted to God our heavenly Father. "What shall I render unto the Lord for all his benefits toward me? *I will take the cup of salvation; call upon the name of the Lord.*" (Ps 116:13)

God Bless you all and have a joyful and thankful Thanksgiving.

2008

Practices for the New Year

Sharon Roundtree-Brewer

I LIKE TO WORK WITH NUMBERS. I don't mean I like solving mathematical problems or things of that sort. (Although I must admit, I was addicted to Sudoku for a while.) What I mean is that I like using numbers to keep track of things. Lately, I have been using numbers to keep track of my nutrition and physical fitness, and I have found the perfect online website to help me with this practice.

I log in on my special website daily and] input the food that I eat. The website provides me with specific numbers on what I have consumed in calories, proteins, fats, calcium, carbohydrates, iron, etc. I get specific numbers; complete with a diagram, on whether I am consuming recommended amounts of nutrients. I also input numbers regarding my physical activities such as walking, tennis and other conditioning. Based on my input the website provides me with specific information on the calories I bum and tells me whether I am on schedule to meet my goals. I certainly do not claim that I have reached the level of fitness and nutrition to which I ultimately aspire, but my practice of keeping numbers helps me enormously to stay on track.

Keeping numbers reminds me how much I also need specific practices to help me maintain a good relationship with God, and overall good spiritual health. What better time could there be to evaluate my devotional and spiritual practices than the beginning of the New Year?

I realize that I cannot maintain a good relationship with God, and live an overall good spiritual life, by merely saying that I'm going to do it. I have to do something specific to make it happen. I have to maintain specific devotional and spiritual practices and constantly remind myself to stay with these practices in order to reach my goals.

The spiritual and devotional practices available to me include prayer, meditation, reading the Bible and other religious or spiritual texts, attending worship, participating in church activities, and serving others. I admit that I am more consistent with some practices than I am with others. For example, I feel that I need to do more reading of the Bible and serving others. On the other hand, I attend worship every Sunday, except rarely, and 1 meditate daily immediately following my morning exercise routine.

I would like to become more consistent overall in my spiritual and devotional practices. I know there are a variety of ways for me to do this, and I will continue to search until I find the specific way that works best for me.

Perhaps you are also evaluating your spiritual and devotional practices at the beginning of this New Year. If so, I wish you well. I pray for the best for you in all of your cares and concerns throughout the New Year and beyond, especially in your relationship with God and in your overall spiritual health.

Six More Weeks of Winter!

Karen Bergenholtz

▲ ▲ ▲

OH DEAR ME, WHAT A SURPRISE!? The groundhog saw his shadow on February 2, and the prediction of course is six more weeks of winter. Are you happy to climb back to hibernation? Or are you feeling buried with the burden of gloomy days, lack of sunshine, and warmth of the sun?

Pardon me if you are a snow lover, skier, or snowboarder but winter in southern New England thus far has been lackluster. Our western states, however, are enjoying terrific snowfalls. With too much snow though comes the fear of avalanches. A recent piece on National Public Radio reported on the danger of avalanches in Colorado, especially on a stretch of highway where a snowplow was buried and its driver Eddie Imel perished. Danny Jaramillo, Eddie's partner, survived however by digging for 18 hours, 20 feet straight up using a flashlight. Amazing.

I'm sure God was with Danny Jaramillo as he dug his way to daylight bringing him energy, determination, persistence, and hope. The idea of someone using a flashlight, an instrument of light, brought me to thinking about God as the giver of Light. No batteries required. No electric bill to pay.

The season of Lent has just begun, where we journey with stories of Jesus' growing ministry; stories of ordinary individuals, some fallen who need something new in their lives. They leave the burrows of the familiar and follow. Leaving darkness and embracing Light. Take yourself back to Jesus' day and imagine how this Light carried forward after the Cross, journeying across time to our day. How did it endure?

Reading the words in Isaiah 58 brings some idea of how Jesus' followers carried his Way forward to us:

> *"Then you shall call, and the Lord will answer; you shall cry for help,*
> *and he will say, Here I am. If you remove the yoke from among you,*
> *the pointing of the finger, the speaking of evil, if you offer your food to*
> *the hungry and satisfy the needs of the afflicted, then your light shall*
> *rise in the darkness and your gloom be like the noonday. The Lord will*
> *guide you continually, and satisfy your needs in parched places, and*
> *make your bones strong; and you shall be like a watered garden, like*
> *a spring of water, whose waters never fail. Your ancient ruins shall be*
> *rebuilt; you shall raise up the foundations of many generations; you shall*
> *be called the repairer of the breach, the restorer of streets to live in."*

ISA 58: 9-12

Isaiah instructs here, how to carry your light, not alone, but with the Lord's presence and guidance "for many generations." Lent is opportunity to start crawling out of our burrows. Just put one paw in front of the other. God is waiting for us.

I'm Ready

Richard Kennedy

AS WE APPROACH THE MOST SACRED OF DAYS on the Christian calendar we find ourselves preparing for the rebirth of Jesus and his triumph over the bonds of death.

Having recently reread the account of the events of Jesus' rebirth found in Luke 24 (KJV) we find that the disciples, the closest to Jesus, were not prepared for this most important event. They were surprised to find the tomb empty.

> **Luke 24:11** *And their words seemed to them as idle tales and they believed them not.*

Then even as Jesus appeared to them they didn't recognize him as their Lord and Savior.

> **Luke 24:16** *But their eyes were holden that they did not know him.*

These men walked with the man they call Rabbi for 7.5 miles and thought him a stranger! Will we know Jesus when we meet Him? Are we prepared for His rebirth? Is Easter a holiday or the most important day of our lives? How do we prepare for this Event? Will we stand next to the Lord and think him a stranger who is out of touch with current events! The disciples didn't know it was Jesus until he broke bread with them as he had so many times before.

Luke 24:35 *And they told what things were **done** in the way and haw he was known of them in breaking of bread.*

Even then, when they should have been joyful and praising that the prophecy had been fulfilled and they were indeed saved, they were terrified.

Luke 24:37 *But they were terrified and affrighted and supposed that they had seen a spirit.*

Will we be terrified also? Or will we know this is a time of Joy and Praise? Will we make this a time of our rebirth and know all our sins are washed away by the blood of Christ? All we have to do is truly accept Christ as our Savior and the Son of God and we will again be as pure as the newborn child and find everlasting Peace.

As for me, I will make myself ready for this Easter. I have found Him, I'm going to live for Christ for the rest of my life. I'm ready. When we as a Church break bread and drink the wine I will know it is my Lord and Savior coming into my presence purifying me once again from the sins of the world and allowing me to forgive the wrongs done against me. And I will praise God for the blessings he has showered on the world.

Luke 24:53 *And were continually in the temple, praising and blessing God. Amen.*

"Oh, the blood of Jesus, Oh, the blood of Jesus; It will never lose its power."

Praise God!

Spring Cleaning for the Soul

Beth O'Sullivan

▲ ▲ ▲

WELL IT IS THAT ANNUAL TIME of year — to clean and purge. But I don't know if you are like me but I have a hard time throwing anything away. My basement is full of books, toys, and file folders of information that I might need "someday". My closet is jam-packed with clothes that I haven't worn in years, but they are too good to throw out or give away.

But there comes time when even a self-identified pack rat like me needs to purge some things; time for spring-cleaning. It's time to get into the closet and toss or recycle. It is time to donate the books, pass along the toys.

Isn't it a wonderful feeling when we've cleaned a room, or an attic, or a cellar and there is room again to move about? It feels like the room can breathe again, and so can we. It is like a new energy flowing! A little feng shui goes a long way and if it works for our physical surroundings, so it can be for our souls.

Spring is a time for new beginnings and new growth; we all have our own little rituals for greeting spring. But it is hard to be born again into new life if we are pack rats and hanging onto all of that old stuff in our hearts, minds and souls. Maybe it is a good time to do a little bit of spiritual cleaning — feng shui for our souls.

We all have times when we get stuck in a rut — but Easter has told us that there are new roads waiting for us. The miracle of springtime has arrived. The earth naturally breaks from the winter's bond, but for humans it is not automatic. Spring cleaning for the souls requires that we get up and do it.

The Easter promise requires us to be Easter people. Discover what we want to change; to decide whether it is something we have the power to change, and to realize what tools the Spirit has given us for making it happen. This means making time for spiritual self-discovery. Step aside from our busy lives, try to relax, listen to your inner voice, and meditate on life.

As David Blanchard has written:

> *Rise up to hope,*
> *Rise up to love,*
> *Rise up to heal,*
> *Rise up to forgive,*
> *Rise up to courage,*
> *Rise up to foolishness*
> *Rise up to wisdom*
> *Rise up, even to die.*
> *But most especially, rise up to life,*
> *Rise up to the love of life and to living life to the fullest.*

The Great Mulligan

Michael Waller

▲ ▲ ▲

SPRINGTIME AND OUTDOOR SPORTS. Iт's time for spring soccer, baseball, softball and that strange game called golf. It's time to enjoy what one TV sportscaster once described as the "thrill of victory and the agony of defeat." No one who has ever played any sport has avoided the frustration of the strikeout… the dropped fly ball… or the missed three-foot putt. It's aaaw-wwaaaaa time! It's when the pitcher wishes he/she had that fat pitch back after watching it zoom out of the park. In golf (while it's not officially allowed, but among hackers it's there anyway) there is the Mulligan…the do-over…. the second chance. It can be a cleansing and a fresh start.

Scripture gives us countless stories of God-given Great Mulligans. They are acts of repentance, of forgiveness, and renewal. There is Nicodemus asking Jesus how he can see the Kingdom of Heaven, and Jesus replies that when he (or we) chooses to be born again in spirit we get a fresh start. A second chance is not one of age, but of choice. We see Nicodemus later in John's gospel as a defender of Christ. He sought, and received renewal. (John 3)

There is the Samaritan woman at the well who gives Jesus water, but also needs and asks him for "living water" so that she will not thirst. She wants and asks for a fresh start. In faith she receives, and calls her townspeople together to proclaim God's power through Jesus. Her faith gives her a do-over (John 4)

The Pharisee Saul makes persecuting new Christians his mission, and he's good at it. But as he travels to Damascus he is stricken by a vision of Jesus calling him to STOP. Saul is blinded. But he is also awakened; he knows he needs a new start to turn away from persecution and to begin anew declaring the power and the hope and the promise of Jesus. Saul becomes Paul; he leads others to belief; he grants others renewal, and offers each of us the gift of the Great Mulligan.... the fresh start as a child of God. (Acts 9)

God's Perfect Plan

Gordon Wolfgang

▲ ▲ ▲

RECENTLY THE MEDIA TOLD A story of a celebrity whose newborn baby had died. When asked how he felt he said 'who am I to question God's perfect plan?' I sat up and took notice. How could one, in the face of such enormous sadness and devastation, drink from the well of spirituality? Was this God's perfect plan?

What about Angel Torres? He was struck down on the streets of Hartford Wednesday by a hit and run driver. The bigger question was why did bystanders not come to his assistance? Why did the cars drive around his inert body? Why didn't the nine people who stood on the sidewalk call 911? He is paralyzed from the waist down. Was this God's perfect plan?

Then there are the other questions. The questions of war, hunger, poverty, murder, torture. How do I reconcile the human condition with God's perfect plan?

I don't have the answers. Some days all I have are questions. What I do have is the ability to remain teachable, the desire to know the difference between self-will and God's will and the willingness to learn what acceptance is.

If self-will is the stubborn adherence to one's own goals and ideas, then I have that. To get myself ready to know God's will I pray to free my heart of people, places and things. Having done this, I try not to go with feelings or impressions lest I make myself liable to false beliefs. I seek reflection, meditation and discussion with others for a. more solid framework. Then it comes down to acceptance—my ability to willingly accept what I cannot change.

So, you may ask, what does this have to do with God's perfect plan? The knowledge of self-will helps me to stay right-sized. Acceptance allows me freedom to make choices that align to the forces of my spirituality. I can't change death; I can mourn. I can share my grief with others. I can't prevent another from leaving the scene of an accident but I can step off the sidewalk. I can pray for Mr. Torres and his family. I can't stop war but I can become an activist. I can't relieve the world's hunger but I can donate time, money, and goods.

I want to be part of God's perfect plan.

The Prayer Zone

Betsy Bascom

Come near to God, and God will come near to you

JAS 4:8

ONE OF THE BEST BOOKS I have read in the past year is The Reading Zone by Nancy Atwell. The main premise of the book is that teachers need to provide many opportunities for their students to become totally immersed in the books they are reading, that they will not become proficient readers unless they are able to get into the "zone." I continue to strive to provide such opportunities for my students. I also encourage them to make connections between the books they are reading and the world around them, something all good readers are able to do.

For the past 2½ years I have maintained a committed time to a morning devotional. First I read a chapter of my Study Bible. I follow this with a reading from *Grace for the Moment*, a small book of inspirational thoughts by Max Lucado. My devotional ends with a prayer and meditation. Since late winter I have been struggling with my devotional, especially with the prayer. I find my mind wandering in a million different directions. I have not been able to immerse myself in a conversation with God. And that's where the connection was made. What I need to do is to enter "The Prayer Zone" when praying and meditating just as I enter "The Reading Zone" when I am engaged in a good book.

In *Grace*, Lucado devotes several of his daily thoughts to prayer. In one he asks. "How long has it been since you let God have you? How long since you gave him a portion of undiluted, uninterrupted time listening for his voice?" He then goes on to reflect on the frequency with which Jesus spent time praying and listening to God, asking, "If the perfect Christ saw the necessity of prayer, wouldn't we be wise to do the same?" Yet another day's thought poses this question: "Is your approach to prayer secondhand? Have you tried to have a daily quiet time and not been successful? Is it easier to let others spend time with God and listen to what they have to say? Since you don't experience other facets of your life secondhand, Lucado entreats, "Why would you want to do so in your relationship with God?"

So, how do we put aside the outside world in order to spend time talking and listening to God, to enter 'The Prayer Zone?"Lucado offers a couple of great suggestions:

- A regular time and place. Select a time in your schedule and a quiet corner in your world and claim it for God
- Allow no intrusions: Turn off the phone, the TV, the radio
- Select a time when your family is occupied in activities of their own
- Come with a listening and open heart. Let God have you spend time listening for and to him

And so summer is here. I love the ease of this time of year I can kick back and take the time to do those things I put off during the school year. I have my pile of books ready and am looking forward to entering "the reading zone." But more importantly, I am looking forward to finding effective ways to put myself into "the prayer zone." where I can truly come near to God and listen to his voice. I hope many of you too will try to find your own time and place to be near to God as well.

Good News and Good News

Sharon Roundtree-Brewer

I DON'T REMEMBER THE EXACT DATE, but it was more than four years ago when the Pastor invited the Board of Deacons to alternate with him in writing cover articles for the *Red Doors*. Since that time, the Pastor has been writing cover articles for the *Red Doors* for the first of each month, and the Board of Deacons has been writing cover articles on the 15th of each month.

As you are aware, our church is no longer publishing the *Red Doors* twice each month. The church has begun to publish our newsletter once each month, and the publication date for each issue is the first of the month. This change becomes effective with this September issue of the *Red Doors*.

With regard to the *Red Doors*, I am pleased to inform you that I have some good news and I have some good news. The good news is that the Pastor will continue to write monthly cover articles for the *Red Doors*. However, since there is only one *Red Doors* each month, the Board of Deacons no longer will be writing cover articles. And the good news is that the Board of Deacons is introducing the Deacons' Corner in this issue of the *Red Doors*. The Deacons' Corner is a page set aside in the *Red Doors* that the deacons will use to share messages of Faith with members and friends of the Middlefield Federated Church.

I believe it is indeed good news that the deacons will continue to share their messages of Faith in the *Red Doors*. But please don't misunderstand me. It is not about the deacons, I believe it is good news when anyone in our congregation, deacon or otherwise, opens up in truth to share with others. As a congregation and church family, we nourish ourselves deeply when we share our Faith journeys with each other. It is nourishing, comforting, and inspiring to hear others talk about their beliefs, their challenges, their growth, their fears, their liberation, and their relationship with God and other people. It is nourishing as well to the individuals who do the sharing when they open themselves up to others.

In addition, when we share our Faith journeys, we not only nourish ourselves or others who may be touched by what we have to say, but we also set an example of sharing that supports and encourages others to tell their stories. Our church has given our members and friends many opportunities to share their Faith with the congregation. We share our Faith during laity Sunday, during August worship service, at Faith Forums, at the church book club discussions, at bible study discussions and in the *Red Doors*. I celebrate our sharing and I give thanks to God for our growth and development as a church family.

I also give thanks to our Pastor for his initial invitation to the deacons to share their messages in the *Red Doors*, and I give thanks for the many other ways that the Pastor and the committees and boards of our church have helped our congregation grow in support of each other by sharing.

Finally, I give thanks to the congregation for your courage, strength, caring, and willingness to share your Faith.

OCTOBER 1

"What Would You Like On Your Tombstone?"

Bergenholtz

ARE YOU FAMILIAR WITH THE TV COMMERCIAL for Tombstone Pizza that asks, "What would you like on your Tombstone?" referring to what topping you would like on your pizza?

In October, children's thoughts often turn to costume schemes; visions of candy Treats and friendly ghosts. In church traditions, old souls are celebrated come All Souls Day in early November, remembering those cherished in life. I have witnessed the celebration of the faith and lives in our church's family, especially in the past year.

Back in the spring, Paul and I visited Concord, walking to Authors Ridge to visit the graves of Alcott, Emerson, and Thoreau. I thought it fitting that Thoreau's grave was known only by a small stone, probably less than one foot tall, marked simply "Henry," for the author whose works are now so widely known, taught and inspire. I wondered about epitaphs of other famous souls, learning that Mahatma Gandhi's reads "Hey Ram" (translated "Oh, God"). Martin Luther King, Jr.'s reads, "Free at last, Free at last. Thank God Almighty I'm Free at Last."

Epitaphs are chosen either before death, or after. Still words carved are by human hand and thought for the benefit of visitors, family, friends and those passing through. I wonder what God would chisel? What would you like God to say?

An Open Prayer

Roger Brewer

▲ ▲ ▲

WHEN I WAS A YOUNG MAN in my mid-twenties living in the city of Hartford, I had a special place in a Hartford city park where I would go to pray. And when I would pray, I would tell God everything. I knew that I could not conceal my thoughts, heart or behavior from God, so I didn't even try. I talked to God about anything and everything and how liberating it was to willingly and completely open my life up to the Almighty God.

One evening as I was praying in that Hartford city park, it occurred to me that I should willingly open my whole life as a continuous prayer. I felt that if God already had knowledge of my every thought and behavior, then why not.

With my whole life open as a prayer, I try to behave as though God is always watching me. This is a good tool to help me in my effort to maintain good thoughts and behavior and avoid self-deception.

But I still cherish the times with God when I can tell it all, even though God already knows it.

Almighty God, I pray that you might help me in my failures and my shortcomings, and forgive me for my sins, each and every one. For those times when I have hurt or offended other people, when I have failed to love my neighbors as I should, when I have lacked the courage to do what is right, when I have been blinded by pride or conceit, or when I have taken the wrong path because of my tears or ignorance, I pray that you might have mercy on me. I pray that you might strengthen me where I am weak and enlighten me when I get caught in my illusions.

Gracious God, I thank you for this life that you have given to me and for all the blessings and opportunities that you have provided. I pray that I might truly live my life as a prayer, with my failures and shortcomings as my confessions of sin and plea for strength and guidance to move beyond, and with any good that I might do that you find pleasing as a testimony of my tremendous thanks and gratitude for your light in my life. Dear God, this is my life and this is my prayer to you. May I always be aware of your presence in my life, now, and forevermore. Amen.

Celebrating Christmas

Roger Brewer

▲ ▲ ▲

JESUS IS GOD'S GIFT TO THE WORLD. How will you be celebrating God's special gift during this Christmas season?

As for me, I will be attending Christmas worship service as usual. I will also engage in special prayer at various times with family and friends.

In addition, I have to admit that I will participate in gift giving, Christmas decorating, Christmas luncheons, Christmas parties, and gatherings with family and friends. I appreciate fully from the Pastor's sermon last year on Sunday, December 2, 2007 that these particular activities, although filled perhaps with joy and generosity, do not focus on Jesus. I pray that I do not get so preoccupied with these activities that I forget the true meaning of Christmas, I pray also that I may experience the presence of Jesus, if only occasionally, in the parties, gift giving and gatherings that I enjoy.

Inspired in part by the Pastor's sermon, I feel strongly that I should extend my Christmas celebration beyond the usual activities I have described. I search this year as I did last year for the most appropriate way to do that.

I ask myself what would Jesus have me do to celebrate his birthday. Unlike many of us here on earth, Jesus certainly does not seek attention on his birthday simply because he likes attention. In my mind, he is too powerful and too secure to crave or need the attention of others. Indeed, during his earthly ministry, he was a humble person who often withdrew intentionally from the limelight.

Knowing Jesus the way I think I know him, I conclude that if he truly wants me to celebrate his birthday, he wants me to do so by devoting myself to a task that he would have me do. Or perhaps he would have me celebrate in a way that benefits my own growth and development, or provide a benefit or service to others.

As I think about it, despite what I may do, Christmas always bring special moments of Insight, perspective, and clarity in my life, and there are occasions during the season when I feel the presence of God in a special kind of way. I give thanks for these gifts and pray that they may continue.

What I should do in total to celebrate Christmas is at the moment a bit unclear to me. But there is one thing about which I am certain. Jesus is God's gift to the world. Let us rejoice and be glad in it.

I wish you, your family, your friends, and all of your concerns the very best during this Christmas season.

2009

▲▲▲

What, Me Worry?

Paul Bergenholtz

AS A CHILD GROWING UP in the early 1960s, I would say that I practically lived a "worry free" life. Depending on the season of the year, I would play football, basketball or baseball with my friends. In the summer, I would fish, swim or ride my bike around town and all without parental supervision. My only concern was that I had to be home by 6 p.m. for supper. It was a great time to be a kid.

However, as I grew older, my "worry free" life began to evaporate, as I became a husband, a father, an active church member and a boss. With all of these responsibilities that come with these titles, there is obviously much to worry about.

I am certain that I am not alone when it comes to worrying about the future. All we have to do is read the newspapers or watch the evening news to see that we live in a very troubled world, especially these days with our country still at war and our economy in the worst shape since the Great Depression. How can one not worry?

However, when I feel overwhelmed or overwrought with worry, I reach for Jesus for solace and he instructs us about worry in Matthew 6: 25-27:

"Therefore I tell you, do not worry about your life, what you will eat or drink; or about your body, what you will wear. Is not life more important than food, and the body more important than clothes? Look at the birds of the air; they do not sow or reap or store away in barns, and yet your

heavenly Father feeds them. Are you not much more valuable than they? Who of you by worrying can add a single hour to his life? "

Only when we allow ourselves to open our hearts, minds and souls to Jesus' teachings, are we then able to free ourselves of the worries that imprison us.

May the coming new year bring peace and comfort to you and your loved ones.

Update on the Board of Deacons
Roger Brewer

▲ ▲ ▲

WHAT IS THE BOARD OF DEACONS and what to the deacons do? The answer to this question is included in the 2008 Annual Report of the Middlefield Federated Church. A brief answer is also included here.

The Articles of Federation of the Middlefield Federated Church provide that the Board of Deacons shall assist the Pastor by acting as spiritual leaders of the Church. With the assistance and direction of the Pastor, the Board of Deacons ministers to the needs of church members and also ministers in the Pastor's absence. Additionally, the deacons nurture their own faith through study, prayer and meetings with fellow deacons and the Pastor.

As examples of specific deacon activities, the deacons serve home communion, assist the pastor in serving communion at the church, conduct visitations, lead worship during the Pastor's absence, facilitate Faith Forums, usher at funerals and memorial services and participate in devotionals.

The Board of Deacons currently meets on the first and third Wednesdays of each month. On the first Wednesdays of each month we hold our devotional meetings. We hold administrative meetings on the third Wednesdays of each month.

With regard to visitation, if you are aware of any members of our congregation who you believe would benefit from deacon visitation and would welcome it, please contact a member of the Board of Deacons.

In addition, if you are aware of someone who is unable to attend church and would like to receive home communion, please speak to a member of the Board of Deacons or call the church office.

The current members of the Board of Deacons are

* Sharon Roundtree-Brewer
* Beth O'Sullivan
* Richard Kennedy
* Betsy Bascom
* Bridget Melien
* Paul Bergenholtz
* Gordon Wolfgang
* Karen Bergenholtz
* Mike Waller
* Millie Simonzi
* Roger Brewer

We ask that you pray for the Board of Deacons in our work. We continue to pray for you, our congregation and friends and indeed all of God's children throughout the world.

Spending Time

Roger Brewer

FREQUENTLY, BUT SURELY NOT OFTEN ENOUGH, I make that 50 to 60 minute drive north to visit my friend who currently resides in a nursing home. Last September, she celebrated her 87th birthday. She is limited now by an assortment of physical health problems. However, in my opinion, she is today just as capable mentally and emotionally as she was when I first met her 40 years ago.

My friend calls me her "son," and I call her my "mom." Years ago her youngest biological son and I hung out together like brothers. But my special relationship with my "mom" stands on its own.

When I visit her, we talk about old times as well as current blessings and concerns. Sometimes I learn things about her that never knew. She gets a few surprises from me also. Whatever we do or say, the true essence of our visits is that we are together. We join hands and we pray for each other.

I am uplifted and nourished tremendously when I visit my "mom." I feel the presence of God with us.

It is likewise when I visit friends and fellow members of our congregation here at the Middlefield Federated Church. And I know that I am not alone in the value that I place on visitation.

Members of the Board of Deacons and other members of our congregation make numerous visits each year to church members and friends. (Caring individuals also send cards, make phone calls, and pray for others.) The visitation that occurs within our congregation is an important strength that we should cherish, honor and continue.

I recently read a daily meditation on visitation that was written by Anthony B. Robinson, a UCC Pastor who teaches leadership at Emmanuel College at the University of Toronto. In his meditation, Pastor Robinson wrote, "As we make or receive a visit to friends and fellow believers, life is at least potentially knit more deeply together and faith strengthened. Moreover, we remember in our visits our God, who in Jesus Christ has 'visited' his people."

I give thanks to the Almighty God for the visitation ministry that is very much alive in our church. I give thanks for the ways in which this ministry nourishes and strengthens those who are visited as well as those who make the visits. I pray that with the blessings of our God that we might enlarge and enrich our visitation and reach our highest potential.

Spring Renewal

Gordon Wolfgang

▲ ▲ ▲

AS I LOOK THROUGH THE WINDOWPANES at my side yard, I see the greening of spring. With the greening comes my desire to be outside and make things clean and tidy. Ahh, today will be MY day. My day to smell the spring air, grab a rake. My day to dig and cut and trim the gardens. My day to make tidy the detritus of fall and winter. My day for renewal and reparation.

In the quiet of the early morning I revel in the ritual. I hear the birds. I smell the soil. I feel the morning chill. This is my day to prepare for the coming of spring.

At day's end, when all my yard work is done, I am at peace.

I am reminded of how alike my day of renewal and reparation is to that of the Lenten season.

Lent, for me, is the preparation of my beliefs; through prayer, praise, requests of guidance and the confessing of sins. These simple, yet significant, acts prepare me for the coming of Christ.

The beauty is that prayer can be done spontaneously and at any moment. Each Easter season I am reminded of my religious roots as I attend church. This culminates in Holy Week; the last week of Lent and the week before Easter. I have prepared myself and am ready for the joyous rituals of Palm Sunday, Maundy Thursday and Good Friday.

Just as the New England soil has been denied nourishment during winter's cold stillness, the Lenten season affords me the act of self-denial (in my case, ice cream!). Though others may practice restraint with respect to actions of body, speech and mind my spiritual the purpose is the same—to recognize that spiritual and religious goals can be impeded by indulgence.

As spring arrives so does Easter Sunday, the celebration of the Resurrection of Jesus Christ. I am blessed to be a part of my church community and a steward of the earth to share these days with you.

Lucky 7

Michael Waller

▲ ▲ ▲

SEVERAL WEEKS AGO I BOUGHT a Connecticut Lottery ticket. You know, one of those scratch-off things. I haven't bought one of them in probably five years. First, I do not recall ever winning, and second, gambling isn't my thing. It's like hoping for something for nothing — well, one buck anyway. This ticket has the name "Lucky 7" with seven chances to win! But I haven't scratched it yet. I am more interested and more challenged by prayer, and by the scriptural urging to ask for God's mercy, his forgiveness, and his direction. These are things that are eternal.

Hymn 405 is a favorite of many—

Seek ye first the kingdom of God, and his righteousness, and all these things will be added unto you — Alleluia.
Ask, and it shall be given unto you — Seek and you shall find;
knock and the door will be opened into you — Alleluia.

This encouragement, and urging is repeated many times in both the Old and New Testaments. In Deuteronomy 4:29-30 as the Jews were about to cross the Jordan River, Moses instructs his people "…from there you will find Him (the Lord) if you search for Him with all your heart and soul".

In Matthew 10:31-33 Jesus teaches the disciples (and us) not to be anxious for what we eat or wear, because "God knows what we need and feeds our faith, telling us to seek first God's kingdom and righteousness and all these things will be added to you." Again, don't give up asking, but be persistent in calling on God (Luke 11:10-13) Jesus tells of the householder who is asked in the middle of the night by a friend for three loaves. At first the householder says it's late, the children are in bed, go away. But the person in need keeps asking and because of this the householder gives what is needed. Note that it says who is needed (but not necessarily what may be wanted). Jesus' parable continues that if a child asks for a fish the father will not give a snake — and if we bestow good gifts to our children, how much more will our Father in Heaven give the Holy Spirit to those who ask.

So when we buy a lottery ticket we're not asking for a blessing. We're hoping for luck. Should we therefore be persistent and buy another ticket next week? Hardly—because in all likelihood we're merely guessing and betting. But we're not asking God from our hearts.

Seek — persistently — for God's kingdom, and God will hear. Knock and it will be open. Trust God.

Now, I'm going to scratch the "Lucky 7". Match any number to the "winning numbers". Let's see, 3... 2... 27... 54... 777... 9... and the lucky number is 22. Oh, well!

Stories

Bridget Melien

THERE'S A CERTAIN WAY THE LIGHT FEELS on a June morning. I can almost run my fingers through it. The smell of rambling roses, the lazy buzz of insects and the earth rising up with warmth transports me back to being an eight year old girl on the farm. All of my senses take me back to my roots at this special time of year, of family and farm, hard work, strawberry shortcake and carrying Granny's tea to the field to quench the thirst of brothers and sisters working alongside Mom and Dad.

These days are precious to me and remind me of the importance of memories and the telling of the stories. The stories of not only our own life experience but the ongoing story of Jesus' life and all that those stories still teach us today 2,000 years later.

This June and throughout the year, take pause with me to remember your stories and the stories of Jesus. Share them with as many as you can as it is in the remembering and the telling that Jesus stays alive within all of us.

Granny Thayer's Tea

Make a pitcher of strong black tea and while still hot, sweeten to taste and add the magic ingredient, fresh spearmint. As it cools but before completely cool, add two or three healthy spoons of frozen orange juice concentrate and a small can of frozen lemonade. Add water as needed and cool till chilled. Serve with lots of ice.

Your Eight Year Old Friend in Jesus, Bridget

Unwrapping Our Gifts I

Betsy Bascom

There are different kinds of gifts, but the same Spirit. There are different kinds of service, but the same Lord. There are different kinds of working, but the same God works all of them in all men.

1 COR 12: 4-6

SIX YEARS AGO I PARTICIPATED IN "UNWRAPPING OUR GIFTS," an 8-week program offered by our Church designed to "activate spiritual lives, gifts and ministries of the laity." The premise of the Unwrapping is that all Christians are ministers, each in their own way, "gifted and called by God to focused Christian action" The participants, through numerous activities and exercises, identify their unique, special gift, which will help in living out their Christianity in everyday life. Included in the program is Bible study, supportive spiritual sharing and meditation exercises. The participants "explore how they can deepen their relationship with God and revitalize the Church" while creating a deep sense of fellowship.

The experience of Unwrapping has been invaluable to me. I reconnected with a childhood friend, forged lasting spiritual and personal relationships and discovered what gift I could bring to our Church, organizing the Evening Bible Study. Other participants also discovered their callings.

To discover what these gifts are you can contact any of the following past participants: B.M., J.S., J.D., D.G., L.H., S. & B.V., D.D., P.B., J.K., J.S., P.K., L.M., V.F., M.A., or D.C & P.C.

This fall the Church will again be offering this exciting program. Look for further information in the weeks to come. If you have any questions, please contact any of the Church members listed above or former leaders the Pastor, Roger Brewer, Sharon Roundtree-Brewer or Beth O'Sullivan. I ask that you prayerfully consider participating. You won't be sorry that you did!

We Are Together

Richard Kennedy

▲ ▲ ▲

EVERY MORNING SHE WAS AT THE DOOR, I didn't see Her, but somehow felt Her presence. So I opened the door and She came in. She'd say "hello" and sit in the kitchen for a while as if to say, " Do you feed your guest? So I'd dutifully feed Her and give Her water. Then go about my business. All day She would sit around the house doing nothing as far as I could tell, just making Her presence felt. I would leave and come home again, sometimes She would greet me, sometimes not. Late in the evening, She would come into the room and climb up to me, nudge my chin four times, knead me in the chest, turn around and sit down with me for a few hours, once in a while saying something of little importance, at least I thought. At bedtime She would go to the door, I would open it and She would leave, gone for the night.

This ritual continued for years — I'd open the door in the morning, She'd come in sit in the kitchen, wait for food and water, lay around the house all day. When I came home She may or may not greet me, later in the evening would climb up nudge my chin four times, knead me in the chest, sit down and talk on occasion, just enough to let me know she was there, and at bedtime get up and go for the night. Sometimes She would stay the night and on those nights would softly walk around the house, periodically calling out to me just to let me know, "I am here, and I love you, do you still love me? " Some nights I would get up and spend time with Her; She would climb up, nudge my chin four times, knead my chest, sit down and say, " all is well, we will be well, we are together."

Times got tough; I went away for a while, coming home for a few days on occasion, and the roles were reversed. She opened the door to me: I sat down and needed nourishment. She knew and came to me, fed me with four nudges to my chin, kneading me in the chest, sitting down beside me and would not leave. She talked more now, first, to scold me for being gone and leaving her alone, then to say, "all is well, we are well, we are together." Then the old ritual would continue. I opened the door; She came in: (You know the rest).

Years passed, every day the same. However, one day She wasn't at the door. She was getting old but still I needed Her, so I searched for her, but couldn't find Her. I thought She left me. I was angry, how could She do this to me? As I drove away I thought I saw Her. I stopped and backed up. IT WAS SHE. "Where have you been?" She calmly said, "Someone else needed me". "But you are mine" I said. She responded by nudging me on the chin four times and saying, "Let's go home." We did and the ritual started again.

A while later it happened again, She disappeared, longer this time, so long I thought this was the end, She would not come back after all this time. The phone rang one day, the person on the other end asked, "Did you lose something very important to you?" I said, "Yes." "I have Her, She is with me and someone told me you were looking for Her. She is not feeling well and wasn't eating, but She is ok. Boy, She loves to talk; I think She was trying to tell me you needed Her." "Yes, I do." She came home, walked into the house, climbed up, nudged my chin four times, kneaded my chest, sat down and said "all is well, we will be well, we are together."

She left a third time. This time I saw Her go. I knew She was leaving and I knew She would not come back. As She left She turned and said, "I am going Home, but don't worry I will be with you always. All is well, we will be well, and we are together. And I will be back for you when it is time."

Recently I had a dream. I was being nudged four times on my chin as I slept. I woke up and She was there, this time She said, " It is time, come with me. I got up and followed reluctantly at first, She got behind me and kneaded me on my legs, pushing and saying, "it is time, come with me, we are going Home, and it is time to rest. All is well, we are well, and we will be together, forever." I turned around bent over and scooped Her up, She nudged my chin four times, licked my cheek, and said, "I AM HERE, AND I LOVE YOU, ALL IS WELL, WE ARE WELL, WE ARE TOGETHER."

I praise you God.

Unwrapping Our Gifts II

Sharon Roundtree-Brewer

▲ ▲ ▲

ON WEDNESDAY, OCTOBER 7, 2009 FROM 7-9 P.M., our church will begin a study group entitled, UNWRAPPING OUR GIFTS. This study group was a whole new kind of study group for our church when it was first offered in 2001 and then again in 2003. It was a great success on both occasions. Recently, several members of our church have been asking about "Unwrapping" and the Board of Deacons thought it was a good time to offer the program again.

The 8-week course, co-led by the Pastor, Roger Brewer, Bridget Melien, and Sharon Roundtree-Brewer, will help us explore the Biblical vision that all Christians (not just the ordained) are MINISTERS, equally gifted and called by God to different kinds of focused Christian action.

We will explore how we can better live our faith in the real world and span the gulf between Sunday morning and the workweek. Through imaginative Bible studies, interesting case studies, guided journaling exercises, and supportive group discussion, we will discover and strengthen our personal ways of ministering to others in our workplaces, relationships, and world.

The course will meet once a week for a period of 8 weeks (excluding the Thanksgiving week). The dates of the course sessions are: October 7, 14, 21, 28, November 7, 11, 18, and December 2, All sessions are Wednesday from 7:00 p.m. to 9:00 p.m. except the fifth session (November 7), which is a Saturday retreat which runs from 9:00 a.m. to 5:00 p.m.

The only requirements for the course are a sense of adventure, a desire to apply one's faith to the workday world, a commitment to attend the scheduled sessions and commitment to do brief homework assignments.

We are hoping to have a good tum-out for this group! Space is limited however since the optimum size for the group should not exceed 17. Therefore if you are interested, let one of the facilitators know as soon as possible.

We believe this group, and future ones like it will have a strong impact on our congregation, helping us to deepen our faith life, our care for each other, and our ministries. Even if you do not usually participate in church study groups, we invite you to consider attending this one! It will be well worth the time!

If you have any questions or want further information, please talk to any one of the facilitators. Their contact information can be found below. An orientation session will also be held after church at 11:30 a.m. on September 20. This will give anyone who is curious about the program another opportunity to get more information about it.

Glorious

Karen Bergenholtz

GLORIOUS, WHEN AUTUMN COLOR COMES INTO VIEW. It's a little early in Connecticut for full-blown display, but into my brain as a description of the other give it time. I got to thinking about that word, glorious, which popped beauty we are privileged to witness here in New England. Where does the word glorious come from, than a version of "glory"?

The Online Etymology Dictionary provides several references: c.1300, "magnificence" from O.Fr.; from Latin, Gloria, "great praise or honor." It goes on to explain that glory was used in "Biblical writing to translate a Hebrew word which had a sense of "brightness, splendor, magnificence, majesty." In the end, glorious translates as "full of glory." Somehow I doubt that our ancestors would appreciate my using "glorious" as a descriptor of autumn leave—save the word "glorious" for praising our Creator.

"Surely the Presence of The Lord is in this place" is one of my favorite hymns, especially the verse: "I see glory on each face." When we come together in—worship, there is a quiet transformation, as we leave behind the busy-ness of our lives. Peace. Love. Faith. Hope. No matter what you do, how much you earn, how smart, old, young, male, female, color, etc., we are on equal ground. And God sustains us, every day.

"A sense of brightness, splendor, magnificence, majesty." Watch for it.

Rise and shine,
And give God the glory, glory
Children of the Lord.

"God is Still Speaking"

Roger Brewer

▲ ▲ ▲

I LOVE THE STORIES AND PARABLES OF THE BIBLE. When I am open to the spirit of God as I should be, these stories and parables come alive in my life and teach, support and comfort me.

The story of Jonah and the fish IS a good example. Jonah did not do what God had directed him to do. As a result, Jonah ended up in the belly of a fish. Like Jonah, there are times in my life when I do not respond to God's call as I should, and I suffer the consequences for my failure.

When I am challenged today by something that God calls me to do, I try to remind myself that I am reliving the story of Jonah and the fish, and that I should apply the lessons of that story to my current situation. If I can do that, I not only have the advice and direction that I need from God, but I am nourished, comforted, and strengthened as well.

The parable of the Good Samaritan is another example. In this parable, Jesus tells us that there was a man who was robbed and beaten by thieves and left half dead on the road to Jericho. A Priest and a Levite walked past this helpless man without stopping to provide assistance. A Samaritan came upon the man, attended to his wounds and took him to an Inn. Like the Priest and Levite, there are times in my life when I walk past people who are in need without stopping to provide assistance. There are also times when I do stop, like the Good Samaritan, and provide assistance.

Whenever I am faced with an opportunity to help others who are in need, I try to remind myself that I am reliving the parable of the Good Samaritan. I try to apply the lessons of that parable to my own life. I try to take full advantage of all the strength and nourishment that the parable has to offer.

Of course, God does not rely solely on stories and parables of the Bible to guide and nourish us. God speaks through other scripture in the Bible and through other means outside of the Bible. However, I feel the need at times to pay special attention to stories and parables, and I am impressed that the stories and parables that God uses to minister to us do not always come from the Bible.

The United Church of Christ reminds us that God is still speaking. Indeed, God is still speaking, using many ways to do so, including the stories that continue to occur in our personal lives.

Our personal stories are the various incidents and occurrences in our lives, both negative and positive, that challenge or impact us in a significant way. I search the personal stories of my life for the message or messages from God. Perhaps other forces or reasons bring these stories into my life, but certainly God uses these stories to teach me important lessons and to strengthen and nourish me in my spiritual journey.

ALMIGHTY GOD, I pray that all of your children, certainly myself included, may hear and understand your voice, and be strengthened, guided and nourished by your Word, wherever it may be found, whether in the personal stories of our lives, the stories, parables and other readings of the Bible, or elsewhere in your great and mighty creation. Amen.

Using Our Gifts in Christian Ministry

Paul Bergenholtz

▲ ▲ ▲

WE ARE IN THE SEASON OF ADVENT. It is a time of family and friends, gifts and giving. It is also a time for all those great Christmas stories like one of my favorites, "A Christmas Story."

"A Christmas Story" is about a boy named Ralphie, who has a burning desire to receive a BB gun for Christmas. Like Ralphie, I also wanted my own BB gun, but my mother, who was not a fan of BB guns, would pull the "tried and true" admonishment that has stood the test of time. I'll not state it here, but it had something to do with impairing ones vision. In spite of my mother's concerns, I finally received a BB gun for Christmas when I was 13 years old. I think my Dad had something to do with that and boy, that was one great Christmas!

Lately, I have been giving much thought about other types of gifts. However, these gifts are not tangible, but rather, gifts that were given to me by God.

Over the last six weeks, I have been participating in a program with 16 other church members called "Unwrapping Our Gifts." The focus of the program is for each person to find his or her own personal and unique gifts. With help from the other participants, we identify each other's gifts and through conversation and prayer, we explore ways on how our gifts may be used in Christian ministry.

However, one thing is very clear, everyone's gifts are valuable and precious in God's eyes, and we are called by him to use these gifts in the service of others. During this season of Advent and beyond, please invest time to unearth your unique gifts. Those around you may be able to offer you valuable insight about your gifts, so listen to them and then offer your gifts to others with an open and loving heart.

May you enjoy a blessed Advent season with family and friends.

2010

▲ ▲ ▲

How God Speaks to Us Today

Roger Brewer

▲ ▲ ▲

BETSY BASCOM LEADS A BIBLE STUDY CLASS at our church in which I am a student. Currently we are studying the prophet Jeremiah. According to the notes in my study guide, Jeremiah did his prophetic work at a time somewhere between 627 B.C.E. and 587 B.C. E. I used to ask whether the life of a prophet such as Jeremiah, occurring so many years ago, is relevant to what is going on in my life today. I don't ask that question anymore. I understand clearly that many challenges faced by the people described in the Old Testament of the Bible are the same challenges we face today.

At our Bible Study session on Monday, December 14, we discussed (among other things) the particulars of how God called Jeremiah to speak God's words to the people of Judah. During our discussion, we spent time exploring how God speaks to us or calls us today to speak or act in our daily lives.

Today, most of us do not hear God's audible voice in direct one-on-one conversations, as did Moses, Jeremiah, and others described in the Bible. Yet, God still speaks to us and calls us to undertake certain tasks or missions.

In our December study session, we identified various ways in which God speaks to us or calls on us today. Here are at least some of the ways we discussed.

Sometimes we hear the voice of God in what others are saying. For example, a sermon on Sunday morning or advice or counsel from a friend or even a stranger could carry a message from God.

Sometimes we hear the voice of God in certain situations in which we find ourselves. For example, a situation may develop where an aging parent with health problems needs a caretaker. God speaks to us in this way calling us to be that caretaker.

Sometimes a need or an opportunity presents itself and invites us to act. At first we don't respond. This need or opportunity continues to presents itself on different occasions, and perhaps in different forms, until we recognize it as God's voice and finally respond.

Sometimes God plants thoughts in our minds or feelings in our hearts and we recognize them as coming from God and act on them accordingly.

You may be aware of other ways God speaks to us that have not been mentioned here. As I write this article, I am reminded of one of the primary teachings of the course *Unwrapping Our Gifts* that was recently offered at our church. I believe, as taught in *Unwrapping Our Gifts,* that God speaks to us by giving us certain gifts. The gift to sing, the gift to comfort others, the gift to do math, the gift to organize and maintain discipline, and the gift to lead and inspire others are a few examples. The very gifts that God gives us are God's command to use those gifts for good and worthwhile purposes.

Of course, when we listen for God's voice, we must be certain that it is God's voice that we are hearing. Otherwise, we could be led astray. What we hear as we make important decisions in our lives is not always the voice of God. Sometimes we may hear the voice of fear or the voice of other concerns and motivations arising out the ego inconsistent with what God would have us do.

ALMIGHTY GOD, I pray that all of your children, certainly myself included, may hear and discern your true voice, and act upon your voice with faith, courage and commitment, in all ways most pleasing to you. Amen.

Love, Valentine's Day, and the Bible

Gordon Wolfgang

IT IS ALMOST FEBRUARY AND I am reminded of that romantic date; February 14. The day of love...Saint Valentine's Day. And, so, I wondered, who was Saint Valentine? Was he a true patron saint? Is he mentioned in the bible? Did he bring romantic love to all those who wished for it? I did my research! According to Wikipedia a saint "is one who is regarded as the intercessor and advocate in heaven for a nation, place, craft, activity, class, or person." Wikipedia goes on to say that the name "Valentine" isn't listed in the earlier Roman martyrs. The feast of St. Valentine began in 496 because of a high regard among men and to honor one "...whose acts are known only to God." Pope Gelasius I was clear that during this time nothing was known about the lives of any of these martyrs. That Saint Valentine appears as a martyr has been connected to February 14 in the following ways; as a priest in Rome, a bishop of Interamna (modern Terni) and/or a martyr in the Roman province of Africa." There is a very old woodcut portrait of Valentine. The text alongside it reads "that he was a Roman priest martyred during the reign of Claudius II ... He was arrested and imprisoned upon being caught marrying Christian couples and otherwise aiding Christians who were at the time being persecuted by Claudius in Rome. Helping Christians at this time was considered a crime. Claudius took a liking to this prisoner -- until Valentinus tried to convert the Emperor -- whereupon this priest was condemned to death.

He was beaten with clubs and stoned; when that didn't finish him, he was beheaded outside the Flaminian Gate."

Next I wanted to see what the Catholic Church might revel about Saint Valentine. According to the Catholic.org website St. Valentine was a Roman martyred for refusing to give up his Christian faith. Archaeologists have un-earthed a Roman catacomb and an ancient church that was dedicated to Saint Valentine. "Saints are not supposed to rest in peace; they're expected to keep busy: to perform miracles, to intercede. Being in jail or dead is no excuse for non-performance of the supernatural. One legend says, while awaiting his execution, Valentinus restored the sight of his jailer's blind daughter. Another legend says, on the eve of his death, he penned a farewell note to the jailer's daughter, signing it, "From your Valentine." Saint valentine is the "Patron Saint of affianced couples, bee keepers, engaged couples, epilepsy, fainting, greetings, happy marriages, love, lovers, plague, travellers and young people." Saint Valentine is most often depicted in pictures with birds and roses.

Ahhh, there is still more. Is Saint Valentine mentioned in the bible? No. Nary a word about Saint Valentine! I got back "Sorry, no results were found for VALENTINE." If I do a search on http://www.kingjamesbibleonline.org/search.php?word=love, I find 547 matches for L O V E !!! One of the first readings that caught my eye was in Leviticus 19:18. "Thou shalt not avenge, nor bear any grudge against the children of thy people, but thou shalt LOVE thy neighbour as thyself: I [am] the LORD." This fits in perfectly with what the children and young adults are learning in My Faith Center - The Great Commandment! "Jesus is in Jerusalem and the question posed to him is 'Which is the greatest commandment?' Jesus' answer is simple and consistent. Love God. Love your neighbor and love yourself." And the Memory Verse— "He answered, 'You shall love the Lord your God with all your heart, and with all your soul, and with all your strength, and with all your mind; and your neighbor as yourself'" Luke 10:27.

Marjee and I were talking about Sunday school. Marjee related some snippets from the younger children when discussing anger. How do you fix a friendship? And a child answered "well, you get in a room and you fix it." Marjee never went to Sunday School so wondered if she had consistently gotten spiritual messages such as these, when it came time to loving her God, and loving her neighbor as herself, if life thus far would have been a walk in the park!

Seriously, there is a message in all of this. And it is simple. In times of adversity or anger when one is questioning their faith or their friendships, you get in a room and you fix it.

Therefore I LOVE thy commandments above gold; yea, above fine gold.

Ps 119:127

Knock, knock...Who's there?

Michael Waller

▲ ▲ ▲

DO WE WONDER WHO GOD IS, and what God is? Where have we come from, and where are our ancestors, and our children and grandchildren? God knows, and God reveals himself in a personal way, if we but listen. God speaks to us sometimes directly, as he did in the Old Testament, and also boldly and repeatedly through Christ. And Christ frequently declares that he is (I AM) the Messiah...God's Son. Here are a few examples worth pondering.

Genesis 28:12: Jacob in a dream sees a stairway resting on earth with its top reaching to heaven and angels of God ascending and descending on it. There above stood the Lord and he said: "I AM the Lord God of your father Abraham and the God of Isaac".

Exodus 3:11,13,14: God calls Moses, who reluctantly responds, "Who am I that I should go to Pharaoh and bring the Israelites out of Egypt? Suppose I go to the Israelites and tell them that the God of your fathers has sent me... and they ask what is his name...what shall I tell them?" God said to Moses, "I AM who I AM. You will say to the Israelites I AM has sent me to you"

Mark 14:61b-62: Again the high priest asked him, "Are you the Christ, the son of the Blessed One?" "I AM", said Jesus, "and you will see the Son of Man sitting at the right hand of the Mighty One, and coming on the clouds of heaven".

Matthew 16:15-16: "What about you - who do you say I AM?" Simon Peter answered, "You are the Christ, the Son of the Living God."

John 6:33-35: "For the bread of life is he who comes down from heaven and gives life to the world." "Sir", they said, "From now on give us this bread." Then Jesus declared, "I AM the bread of life."

John 8:58: "I tell you the truth," Jesus answered, "before Abraham was born I AM."

John 11:24-25: Martha answered, " I know he (Lazarus) will rise again in the resurrection at the last day." Jesus said to her, "I AM the resurrection and the life."

Rev. 22:13: "I AM the Alpha and the Omega, the first and the last, the beginning and the end."

Who's there? God, please help us hear.

Rest for Your Soul

Betsy Bascom

THIS YEAR THE EVENING BIBLE STUDY GROUP is exploring the book of Jeremiah. As you may or may not know, Jeremiah was a prophet called by God:

> *"Before I formed you in the womb I knew you, before you were born*
> *I set you apart; I appointed you as a prophet to the nations."*

JER 1:5

Jeremiah was God's spokesman to the region of Judah, the last remnant of the chosen land. Unfortunately, when Jeremiah spoke, no matter how eloquently or passionately, no one listened. But Jeremiah never gave up. For 40 years he faithfully proclaimed the word of God.

While reading in preparation for one of the Bible study classes, I came across this verse:

> *This is what the Lord says,*
> *"Stand at the crossroads and look;*
> *ask for the ancient paths, ask where the*
> *good way is, and walk in it; and you*
> *will find rest for your souls."*

JER 6:16

Recently I began reading a new daily companion during my morning devotional called *Trail Thoughts*. The author, Eric Kampmann, uses this same verse as anchor for the book. Later he references it when writing about the "life-long journey we embark on to reach the summit of the holy hill."

God has marked out the path we are to take. Throughout our lives we meander down his path. Often, however, we take side trips down roads we assume will be more pleasurable and rewarding, discovering too late that we have made a mistake. We search once again for God's path, praying that this time we will not be misled and trusting that God will lead us to peace and rest for our souls that he promises.

Jesus states in Matthew 11:29, "Take my yoke upon you and learn from me for I am gentle and humble in heart, and you will find rest for your souls."

We can choose to ignore the Word of God, finding our own wayward paths or, as Jeremiah and Jesus said, we can choose the way of the Lord trusting that he will lead us and we will find rest for our souls.

I wish you peace and rest for your souls.

"Let"

Mike Satagaj

I LOVE DRIVING. IT RESEMBLES to me a video game, with speed and subtle, almost effortless adjustments and somehow I connect it to a small piece of heaven. I have shared with my closest friend my hope that "the" heaven will contain a vast expanse of open road. She doubts that such phenomena exists, and instead reminds me of my lack of that wonderful virtue called patience. And while I maintain that the subjects are mutually exclusive, I must plead no contest to the impatience charge, for in that arena, I am guilty. In fact, I would posit that most of us are guilty.

In the first chapter of James, the author exhorts us to "Let patience have its perfect way with you, that you may be perfect and complete, lacking nothing." The key word in this piece of wisdom is "Let". It is not often easy to "let", for in "letting" you relinquish control, you allow, you cede. The act can be difficult for us, eliciting fears of undesired results while contradicting the basic human penchant for freedom. But it is not an insurmountable habit.

If I may draw an illustration from yet another passion of mine, I coach young hockey players that certain situations sometimes dictate that it is beneficial to 'hold' the puck, and then deliver it on their terms. This strategy may require my player to experience discomfort as he allows his opponent to approach, yet the vacated area provides opportunity for our team to advance. Wayne Gretzky's Hall of Fame career centered around 'holding' the puck. He trusted what he could control (his talent), yet also what he couldn't.

I would argue that what he couldn't control and what we can't control are essentially the same thing and that they belong to the Lord. Somehow, we must trust. Perhaps your ability to 'let' will flourish when you can visualize God in your child's attention span or in your wife's headache or in your boss's production demands or in every driver that sits in the traffic jam or...

JUNE 1

Being a Christian
Roger Brewer

▲ ▲ ▲

ACCORDING TO SCRIPTURE, "...IT WAS in Antioch that the disciples were first called Christians." *Acts 11:26.*

If someone were to ask me today if I am a Christian, I would answer, "Yes, I am a Christian." Indeed, I am a Christian. But in the minds of some, am I really? I may not qualify based on what some may expect of Christians.

I have been thinking a lot lately about what might be an appropriate definition of a Christian. I think of possibilities but nothing comes to mind that really works for me.

I have considered several definitions. Here's one that I found on the Internet: "A Christian is a follower of Christ; one who professes belief in Jesus as the Christ and follows his teachings." At first glance, who would argue with this definition? But what does it mean to profess a belief in Jesus as the Christ? Am I required only to say I believe Jesus is the Son of God? Or must I also know the story of Jesus' life here on earth? If so, how much of that story must I know and accept? And what does it mean to follow his teachings? Must I follow all of his teachings or just some? If only some, how can I identify those that are crucial? And which of the various interpretations of Jesus' teachings must I follow?

You see the problem, don't you? The definitions of a Christian seem themselves to need definitions.

Of course, we could say a Christian is anyone who says he or she is a Christian. If we adopt that definition, we wouldn't need other definitions to define it. All we'd need to know is whether someone said he or she is a Christian. But wait minute. This definition is precise enough, but I still don't like it. Under this definition, anybody could be a Christian. Don't you agree that you should not be able to say you're a Christian until you start believing as a Christian and living the Christian life, whatever that might mean?

Now I'm not saying we should have a Christian police, or anything like that, who gives out tickets to anyone who claims—without justification—that he or she is a Christian. But still there ought to be some accountability, even here on earth.

I have to calm myself down. And when I get quiet on the inside and open my heart to God, I see that I have created a problem where there is in fact no problem in the first place. Don't get me wrong. I love being in fellowship with others who share my beliefs about Jesus and who are committed as I am to follow Jesus' teachings. But it seems to me, that when all is said and done, God looks at the heart and not at the label.

When I get quiet on the inside and open my heart to God, God's asks not whether I am a Christian, but instead what is the quality of my relationship with God.

Almighty God, I pray that you might help me in my confusion, that you might shine a light in my darkness, and guide me always in my need. I pray that it might be so also for all of your children. Amen.

Digital Junkie
Bridget Melien

▲ ▲ ▲

I'LL ADMIT IT; I'M A TOTAL DIGITAL JUNKIE. I've got a Facebook page, I tweet and follow other tweeters; I have two side-by-side monitors, a blackberry, iPod and a lot of other digital stuff. I'm rarely not connected to something. And worst of all, one of the first things I do in the morning is look at my blackberry while still in bed. But maybe this is a redeeming thought and something that might help you other junkies too. Usually the very first thing I look at is a daily devotional that I subscribe to through UCC. Here's a recent one that I liked a lot.

Mind Your (Own) Business

Excerpt from John 21:20-22: "Peter turned and saw the disciple whom Jesus loved following them . . . When Peter saw him, he said to Jesus, 'What about him?' Jesus said to Peter, 'If it is my will that he remain until I come, what is that to you? Follow me!"

Reflection by Anthony B. Robinson

The Gospel of John ends on this wonderfully human note. Peter, who had just been commissioned by the Lord to feed and tend his flock (kind of a big job), notices another disciple referred to in John as "beloved" and asks "What about him?" It would be hard, don't you think, to have one disciple who was apparently loved in a special way by Jesus. Kind of like feeling that our parents love one of our siblings more than they love us (which of course everyone does).

Jesus' response to Peter is nothing if not direct. He pretty much says, "Not your business. You have your task, your work. Pay attention to that. Mind your (own) business."

It's pretty easy to get hooked into minding other people's business, especially if we feel their lot in life is better or more favored than our own. It's easy to ask, aloud or inside, "What's up with that? What about him? Why do I have to do this and she doesn't? Why does he get all the breaks?"

Well, for one thing, we really don't know if he or she does get all the breaks. We don't know what it's like to be that other person. Their path in life may look easier or better than our own, but we don't really know that. More importantly, Jesus tells Peter his job is to mind his business, which is the business of following Jesus as he has been called to do. It's wise counsel. Pay attention to your own discipleship, your own God-given work. Leave the business of others to them and the Lord.

Prayer

Dear God, when I am tempted to make someone else's business my own, call me back to the work and challenges that you have given me. Help me today to pay good attention to my own business. Amen.

So although I am a junkie, one of the good things the Internet does is provide me with access to wonderful resources, and creates a built in devotional time for me each day. Time to ponder, think, pray and be in conversation with God. If you are a digital junkie like me, I hope this resource might create that same space and time for you. Here's the link you can use to sign up for the daily devotional at www.ucc.org. If you are not a digital junkie, I am wishing you the best in creating or staying with your own devotional time in your own way. Enjoy talking with God.

Quiet Time: Relax, Request, Read

Richard Kennedy

Search me, O God, and know my heart; test me and
know my anxious thoughts. See if there is any offensive
way in me, and lead me in the way everlasting.

PSALM 139:23-24 (NIV)

I SHARE WITH YOU A SIMPLE PLAN to have meaningful quiet time with God:

1. Wait on God (*Relax*) -- Be still for a minute; don't come running into God's presence and start talking immediately. Follow God's admonition: "Be still and know that I am God" (Psalm 46:10; see also Isaiah 30:15; 40:31). Be quiet for a while to put yourself into a reverent mood.
2. Pray briefly (*Request*) – Say a short opening prayer to ask God to cleanse your heart and guide you into your time together. Two good passages of Scripture to memorize are:

*"Search me, O God, and know my heart; test me and
know my anxious thoughts. See if there is any offensive
way in me, and lead me in the way everlasting"*

(PSALM 139:23-24; see also 1 JOHN 1:9).

"Open my eyes that I may see wonderful things in your law [the Word]*"*

(PSALM 119:18; see also JOHN 16:13).

You need to be in tune with the Author before you can understand his Book!

3. Read Scripture (*Read*) -- This is where your conversation with God
    begins. He speaks to you through his Word, and you speak with him
    in prayer. Read your Bible

    ...Slowly. Don't be in a hurry; don't try to read too large an
    amount; don't race through it.
    ...Repeatedly. Read a passage over and over until you start to
    picture it in your mind. The reason more people don't get more
    out of their Bible reading is that they do not read the Scriptures
    repeatedly.
    ...Without stopping. Don't stop in the middle of a sentence to
    go off on a tangent and do a doctrinal study. Just read that section
    for the pure joy of it, allowing God to speak to you.

*Remember that your goal here is not to gain information, but to feed on the Word
and get to know Christ better.*

(This devotional is adapted from
Rick Warren's Bible Study Methods.)

Prayer Program

Roger Brewer & Sharon Roundtree-Brewer

"The prayer power has never been tried to its full capacity. If we
want to see mighty wonders of divine power and grace wrought in
the place of weakness, failure and disappointment, let us answer
God's standing challenge. 'Call unto me, and I will answer thee, and
show thee great and mighty things which thou knowest not!'"

(J. HUDSON TAYLOR)

HOW TRUE THIS IS! PRAYER has the power to comfort us or rescue us from all of our trials and tribulations. Still, we suffer anxiety, failure, illness, disappointment and many other challenges, great and small, without taking advantage of every opportunity to come together to pray. Prayer is an awesome power and is available to each and every one of us. We can tap into that power by reaching out and calling on God.

Beginning on Thursday, September 16, 2010, the Board of Deacons will begin offering a small group prayer program. The program will be held on the third Thursday of each month and will be offered at 1:00 p.m. and 7:00 p.m. each third Thursday. There are no attendance requirements. Attend whenever you can. We will gather in the meeting room upstairs at the church. The program will not run more than one hour.

There will be a specific format for the program, but basically we will come together to pray for others, ourselves, each other, and issues and situations of concern to us around the world. We will pray for family, friends, neighbors, strangers, our church, our community, our state, our country, and the world in which we live. We will pray for protection, prosperity, healing, achievement, reconciliation, forgiveness and peace. We will also give thanks and praise the almighty God. Essentially, we will come together to talk to God about whatever fears or feelings of gratitude that we might have.

Please come and join us in this program of prayer. No sign-up is necessary. This program is open to all who wish to attend. Please contact Roger Brewer or Sharon Roundtree-Brewer of the Board of Deacons if you have questions. We hope to see you there.

OCTOBER 1

Bees

Karen Bergenholtz

WELL, WE HAD AN INTERESTING WEEKEND here in our neighborhood. Next door to our house has been a huge, maybe two hundred year old ash tree. Problem is, there's been no green growth on it for a couple of years, and wind brings dead, decaying branches on to the road, close to power lines or onto our lawn. It's been tagged for trimming or total takedown over the past year, so I wasn't surprised to find on returning home this past Friday, that the top half of the tree had been surgically removed, with large limbs and trunk pieces scattered about our neighbor's lawn. I assumed the job wasn't finished—there was still about 30 feet of tree standing. Say goodbye to the spooky old tree.

From our kitchen window though, I noticed cars pulling over, with drivers staring at the limbs lying around the ground. I thought, hasn't anyone seen a tree taken down before, sure it's huge, but not worth taking pictures of. A while later, I noticed our neighbor outside taking pictures, so I ventured over. Not only was the tree finished, so was the beehive that was inside the trunk, half on the ground in a piece of the trunk, the remainder still in the tree. Chain-sawed right through, big old tree, and beehive. Thousands of honeybees confused flying about, caused the tree surgeons to quit a little early on Friday. Saturday brought a beekeeper that smoked the hive and scooped most into a cardboard box, hundreds of determined honeybees still trying to get their work done, with the prediction that the queen was still up in the remaining tree, with workers buzzing in and out.

Now, my intention wasn't to write about a disrupted beehive here. But the bees flying around so confused and distraught, with the queen probably right where she's always been, seemed to me what our lives can be like when not centered on our God. We can fly around, multi-task, busy bees, thinking our work is so important here. I can imagine how orderly the bee's world is when all is well, but how out of order and chaotic when removed from the hive environment and the center of their world, they just fall apart.

Over the past summer I decided to somehow center myself daily, and I've always admired Betsy Bascom's decision to read the Bible straight through, at least a chapter a day. When I had participated in the Disciple program a few years back our ambitious schedule took us through the Bible in less than a year. Getting back to basics, one chapter (at least) at a time, doesn't that sound do-able, even with it taking more than a year? It may take me less time to read a chapter than to brush my teeth morning and night (Does this speak badly of my oral hygiene, my dedication, or my slow reading?) Whoever wants to join me, let's start November 1. If you need a bible, call me. Let's get centered.

I Don't Know Where That Came From

Roger Brewer

"GOD SPEAKS TO US IN MANY WAYS." We say it often and how true it is.

Have you ever had one of those occasions when an insight or an understanding suddenly enters your mind, and you say to yourself, "I don't know where that came from?" I'm not referring to just any insight or understanding but a special insight or understanding with distinct characteristics.

As far as I can tell, this insight or understanding about which I write does not come from any prior thought or reasoning process that you may have entertained. It just suddenly appears in your conscious mind. You know that it did not originate with you. Thus, we say, "I don't know where that came from." Despite what you might say, however, you do know where it came from. Deep inside you know it came to you as a gift from God.

Sometimes this special insight or understanding comes to you suddenly when you're struggling with a difficult personal problem. Sometimes it comes to you when you're doing a chore, taking a walk, or doing much of nothing at all. Sometimes it comes to you when you are in conversation with another person.

This insight or understanding from God feels "right" when you get it. It is powerful but not burdensome. Indeed, it is enlightening and liberating. It stands alone and does not depend on other things. It needs no justification. By its truth it is self-sufficient.

As you might expect, I talk to my wife Sharon about situations that trouble me. Sometimes we find ourselves going back and forth in the reasoning process trying to find an answer. On more than one occasion, as we have attempted to reason through a situation, Sharon has blurted out an insight or understanding that is a perfect resolution. And she inevitably says, "That didn't come from me." And we'd look at each other and both know it came from God.

On more than one occasion, I have also found myself blurting out an insight or understanding to someone. On these occasions, I know immediately that it did not come from me. It comes through me as a gift from God to someone else.

"The voice of the Lord is powerful, the voice of the Lord is full of majesty." Psalm 29:4

ALMIGHTY GOD, I pray that I may stay open to all of the ways that you speak to me, including the sudden insight and understanding from you that suddenly appear in my conscious mind. I pray this for all of your children. May we hear your voice always and be comforted and guided eternally by your word. Amen.

Are You Uncomfortable Yet?

Paul Bergenholtz

ONCE AGAIN, I AM WAITING UNTIL THE LAST MINUTE to do something that I should have started a few weeks ago. I have procrastinated, dragged my feet and made excuses (to myself) why I can't finish my task on time. I am starting to get a little stressed.

Each month, one of the deacons volunteer to write an article for the Deacon's Corner and mine is due into Roger Brewer by November 17th. I am writing this article on November 17th. I have asked myself why I volunteered to write this article in the first place. I am not a talented writer. The words do not always come out right and I have been known to place punctuation in the wrong spot. The other deacons are much better writers; I should have let them volunteer to write this article. Let me do those things that I am comfortable with and let the others do those tasks that make me anxious. I don't want to feel uncomfortable. However, that is the theme of my message. Do you feel uncomfortable when your church places an opportunity in front of you?

I am certain that I am not the only person that practices the "art of avoidance" when an opportunity arises. Have you ever thought or stated the following when offered an opportunity by your church?

* *Why me? There are other more qualified people who can do this.*
* *I do not know anything about the task or mission that I am being asked to undertake.*

- *I am not smart enough or talented enough to do the things that need to be done.*
- *I do not feel like it. Translation, "The thing you are asking me to do scares me."*

I am certain that we all have felt this way, but don't feel bad, even Moses had his doubts. After all, didn't he plead with God to let him out of his mission? So you see; you are in pretty good company. Remember, God is always with you to provide strength and direction when you undertake the difficult, the challenging and the uncomfortable.

So here is my offer. Undertake a task or duty that that makes you uncomfortable. It doesn't have to be a big thing, just take a small step and then take another one. The key is to start. If you put your focus on God instead of your "perceived" shortcomings, your confidence will grow and your "self-imposed" limitations will begin to fade away. Our Lord and Savior calls us to be active Christians, so let us get uncomfortable together.

2011

JANUARY 1

Opportunities from God

Bridget Melien

Be kindly affectionate to one another with brotherly love,
in honor giving preference to one another; not lagging
in diligence, fervent in spirit, serving the Lord;

ROM 12: 10-11 (NKJV)

IT'S 8:37 A.M., IT'S SATURDAY MORNING, it's cold and I'm rushing. Worrying that someone might claim my favored real estate in the hot mom (yoga, that is). I notice a gathering of three or four folks at the corner, but just barely, they're only an impediment to me getting there faster. But I do notice a woman as I get closer, I can't tell if she is with the other people or not. She's short, dressed in a winter coat, probably 60ish. As I am almost on top of them, she starts to speak, and has something in her hand. I recognize a strong eastern European accent and the something she has in her hand is a piece of paper. I literally blow right by her, intent on myself and claiming what I think is rightfully mine (ha).

I cannot get her out of my mind, I have even cried over the incident more than once. What was her story that I missed, what was the opportunity that God presented to me that I ignored? To give someone comfort? To give some-one directions? To touch her hands and connect? What did she need that I might have provided? And why did God put her right in front of me?

Was it to move me outside of myself? To look beyond my own desires. No they are not needs, just desires. And I didn't listen, to God, to the best in myself, I just kept on going. And I've been kicking myself ever since. And who knows, maybe she was just looking for money, but I can't help thinking that I missed an opportunity, a God opportunity.

As you welcome this New Year, and if you don't believe in, or haven't made any New Year's resolutions, come with me, step outside yourself and commit to not let these opportunities, whenever and wherever they happen, go by. It's what God wants . . .

Nourished by Scripture
Betsy Bascom

▲ ▲ ▲

THE DEACONS MEET TWICE A MONTH. The first meeting of the month is a devotional led by one of us. Several months ago it was my turn to lead the monthly devotional. I decided that I would ask the Deacons to bring three of their favorite Bible verses to share with the group. The selections chosen were varied and, amazingly, there were no duplicates! It was an enlightening evening. The readings were described as being especially meaningful, inspirational, comforting, instructive, empowering, reflective, uplifting and affirming.

My choices were:

This is what the Lord says:
"Stand at the crossroads and look;
ask for the ancient paths,
ask where the good way is, and walk in it,
and you will find rest for your souls…"

JEREMIAH 6:16

The Lord your God is with you,
He is mighty to save.
He will take great delight in you,

He will quiet you with his love,
He will rejoice over you with singing.

Zephaniah 3:17

But Ruth replied, "Don't urge me to leave you or to turn back
from you. Where you go I will go, and where you stay I will
stay. Your people will be my people and your God my God.
Where you die I will die, and there I will be buried."

Ruth 1:16-17

There are many more verses I could have chosen, but I find great peace, love and commitment to my faith when I read and reflect on these three. I find myself returning to them often, especially when I find my faith wavering.

My Bible is full of highlighted scripture. During my daily devotional, depending on my mood, I highlight verses that have particular meaning to me in my relationship with God. They include words of forgiveness, saving grace, faithfulness, love, joy and a call to action to name only a few.

What are your favorite or most meaningful pieces of scripture? I hope that you too find comfort, enlightenment, affirmation and inspiration in your choices.

Why I Believe in "Sweet Hour of Prayer"

Roger Brewer

"SWEET HOUR OF PRAYER" IS A PRAYER PROGRAM sponsored by the Deacons. We hold two prayer sessions on the third Thursday of each month. One session begins at 1:00 p.m. and the other begins at 7:00 p.m. Both are the same. Neither lasts longer than one hour. You can choose the session that best suits your schedule.

We use a prayer book in our program. When we get requests from others to pray for specific individuals, we enter the names of these individuals in our prayer book. Sometimes we enter the names of individuals that come to us out of our own contemplation.

At our prayer sessions, we lift up specific people we have on our minds by calling out their names. In addition, we call out the names of people listed in our prayer book. We also call out our own names.

We pray for members and friends of our church, friends outside of our church, family members, neighbors, acquaintances, fellow Americans, and our brothers and sisters throughout the world. We pray not only for people who are facing specific challenges in their lives, but also for people who are doing well. We pray for their protection and continued strength and well-being.

We pray for our church and other entities and organizations about which we care. We pray for issues and state of affairs that concern us.

I have heard others say, and I agree, that prayer is any communication that you have with God. As such, prayer is essential to my relationship with God. If I cannot hear God's words or talk to God about what's going on in my life, there is no relationship.

When I pray for someone, I believe my praying makes a difference in that person's life and in my own life as well. I feel that if I can make a difference in my life and in the lives of others simply by praying, then I must.

Often I pray alone. But scripture teaches us that when two or more are gathered in God's name, God is among them. (Matthew 18:20) "Sweet Hour of Prayer" is an important opportunity for members and friends of our church to come together, in addition to our regular worship on Sunday mornings, to talk to God. In my opinion, of all the things that we do in our church community nothing can be much more important than coming together to talk to our Almighty God.

If possible, please join us on the third Thursday of each month for the 1:00 p.m. or the 7:00 p.m. prayer session. If you cannot join us physically, please try to be in prayer wherever you are, for at least 5, 10 or 15 minutes, at the same time that we are holding one of our prayer sessions at the church. If you are praying with us at the same time, though not with us physically, surely your presence will be felt.

The Gift of Laughter

Michael Satagaj

Surely God does not reject one who is blameless or
strengthen the hands of evildoers. He will yet fill your
mouth with laughter and your lips with shouts of joy

JOB 8:20-21

AS CHRISTIANS, WE WOULD HAVE AN EASY TIME IN COM-
PILING A LIST of recent events that qualify as sobering and unjust. From
the natural disasters that struck Japan to the endless disputes that plague the
Middle East to the economic reckoning taking place within our own borders
to the afflictions that wage against the health of many that are close to us, we
are not immune to the effects. Daunting and painful as they may be, we often
have no control over their happenstance or the resulti.ng consequences. Yet
Scripture exhorts us to keep faith. The story of Job provides a relevant example. Though offered through an unwarranted scolding, the above passage still
bears wisdom. It was dictated by Bildad the Shuhite to Job during a conversation that questioned how God might allow his most devout follower to suffer
devastating loss. It is the second verse that I draw particular attention to. For
while none of us are blameless, none deserve tragedy, and we surely know
that Jesus ransomed us from rejection. Disasters, disagreements and death are
inevitable. *"He will yet fill your mouth with laughter...."* Even as it suggests a

triumphant end, it also acknowledges that laughter is a gift. A gift, I witness, that is not a prize bound to success but is free to lift us at any time. It can be medicine. It can be music. At times it is relationship. At times it is contagious. It can break tension between strangers, or deepen the bond between the oldest of friends. It can help ease a burdened soul or carry encouragement or express fondness. Tell me that you have not split your sides to a favorite sitcom or enjoyed a playful tease from your spouse. Tell me you've not laughed to tears over the stupidest of reasons. Maybe they weren't so stupid after all.

Seems a group of scientists were all sitting around discussing which one of them was going to go to God and tell Him that they didn't need him anymore. One of the scientists volunteered and soon found Him.

The scientist says to God — "God. You know. A bunch of us have been thinking and I've come to tell you that we really don't need you anymore. I mean, we've been coming up with great theories and ideas. We've cloned sheep, and we're on the verge of cloning humans. So as you can see, we really don't need you"

God nods understandingly and says. "I see Well. No hard feelings. But before you go, let's have a contest. What do you think?"

The scientist says. "Sure. What kind of contest?"

God: "A man-making contest." The scientist: "Sure! No problem."

The scientist bends down and picks up a handful of dirt and says. "Okay, I'm ready!"

God replies, "Oh, no, no....go get your own dirt."

May each of you laugh hard today. Unsparingly.

Exploring Faith

Karen Bergenholtz

HERE'S AN EQUATION:

16 youth + 1 Pastor + 5 adults* + 1 Anti-Workbook + 21 weeks = 1 confirmation exploration process

If it were that simple! Left out of this mathematical example is the human side of exploring faith, considering difficult questions:

Who wrote the Bible, God or human?

Can someone lose his or her salvation?

Why does God let bad things happen?

Why should I follow Jesus, can't I just say I believe in him?

Is the journey hard? Yes. Is it fun? Mostly. Do we have all the answers? Who do you think we are - God?

We've probably been flying under most people's radar over the past 21 weeks, meeting after church for sessions lasting about one and a half hour. On June 4 youth will commit themselves to joining the church. Let me repeat: on June 4 youth will commit *themselves* to joining the church.

I ask you all to try to recall your own confirmation, and to be in prayer for these young people. They live in a complex world, and deserve our thoughts, prayers and support.

Here's another Equation:

> *"If you have any encouragement from being united with Christ, if any comfort from his love, if any fellowship with the Spirit, if any tenderness and compassion, then make my joy complete by being like-minded, having the same love, being one in spirit and purpose."*

PHIL 2: 1-2

If + If + If + If = Then

*Richard Kennedy, N.B., Bridget Melien, Sharon Roundtree-Brewer, Karen Bergenholtz

The Rubber Duck

Richard Kennedy

▲ ▲ ▲

A CONFIRMATION CLASS HAS JUST BEEN COMPLETED and sixteen young people have committed their life to the service of God. As a group we grew together, discovered together, laughed together and shared "POW, POW, POW" and "quack, quack" every week. These became our chant.

On confirmation Sunday all confirmands and mentors were given a fluorescent rubber duck to be a reminder of the experience we shared and the journey we traveled. The duck is fluorescent so it can be seen in the "dark" when needed the most so we will know the Spirit of the Lord was with us during our journey and will with us on all future journeys This message has become even more important in recent months due to events that have occurred in our community.

I have been blessed over the years to see many children grow from babies to adults. I have been proud of my little contribution in that growth and therefore consider all of them my children. I keep track of them, am proud of their accomplishments and share in their failures. So to lose one of my children because they feel there is nowhere to turn, no one to go to, no hope for them, I feel I have failed to spread the message.

The message that God is always present, that the Holy Spirit is always with you and in you and in everyone around you. All you need do is reach out, open your Soul, let the Grace of God give you peace, and the power to overcome all adversity regardless of how hopeless things may seem.

Twenty-one of us shared a journey together. Confirmation is the beginning. We are bound together in the good times but most especially during the times of despair. Please, know you have twenty-one people with rubber ducks to turn to, all with the Holy Spirit just waiting to reach out to you with God's Hand to lift you up and guide you through the Darkness.

> *"And God will wipe away all tears from their eyes; and there shall*
> *be no more Death, neither sorrow, nor crying, neither shall there*
> *be anymore pain; for the former things are passed away."*

REV 21-4

Forgiveness

Paul Bergenholtz

▲ ▲ ▲

STUDIES SHOW THAT PEOPLE WHO FORGIVE ARE HAPPIER and healthier than those who hold resentments. Based on my experience, I would say this statement is true and I believe many people would agree with me. However, if we believe that people who forgive others tend to live happier and healthier lives, then why don't we forgive others more freely? Don't we all want to be happier and healthier?

Unfortunately, the act of forgiveness does not come easy and our natural instinct is to recoil in self-protection when we've been wronged or hurt and often the ones closest to us are at the center of our hurt. However, our inability to forgive keeps the pain alive and we become prisoners of our own resentment, anger or bitterness. The Bible has much to say about forgiveness, which I will share several passages here:

Matthew 18:21-22
Then Peter came to Jesus and asked, "Lord, how many times shall I forgive my brother when he sins against me? Up to seven times?" Jesus answered, "I tell you, not seven times, but seventy-seven times." (NIV)

Colossians 3:13
Bear with each other and forgive whatever grievances you may have against one another. Forgive as the Lord forgave you. (NIV)

Why must we forgive others when wronged, hurt or slighted? We forgive because Jesus commanded us to forgive, but we also learn from Scripture that if we don't forgive, neither will we be forgiven. Jesus' command is in place for our own good, and we receive the reward of our forgiveness … freedom.

I will leave you with words found in our hymnal, Hymn #390 entitled "Forgive Our Sins as We Forgive," which were written in 1966 by Rosamond E. Herklots.

"Forgive our sins as we forgive," you taught us, Lord, to pray; but you alone can grant us grace to live the words we say.

How can your pardon reach and bless the unforgiving heart that broods on wrongs and will not let old bitterness depart?

In blazing light your cross reveals the truth we dimly knew: what trivial debts are owed to us, how great our debt to you!

Lord, cleanse the depths within our souls, and bid resentment cease; then, bound to all in bonds of love, our lives will spread your peace.

Music That Moves the Spirit

Sharon Roundtree-Brewer

▲ ▲ ▲

DURING THE MONTH OF SEPTEMBER, the deacons will be involved in a few activities to help the congregation get better acquainted with who we are and what we do. We will make available to the congregation a small booklet that includes a short narrative from each deacon explaining what it means to him or her to be a deacon. In addition, one of our deacons will take a few minutes during worship on Sunday, September 11 to share on this same topic. The deacons will also host fellowship hour on September 18. On September 25, while our Pastor is away, the deacons will lead the congregation in worship.

There is one other activity in which the deacons will be involved during the month of September, and I want to take some time now to explain that to you. As some of you are aware, the Board of Deacons holds two meetings each month—a devotional meeting on the first Wednesday of each month and an administrative meeting on the third Wednesday of each month. One of the devotional meetings earlier this year centered on music. Richard Kennedy was the deacon responsible for this particular devotional, and he asked each member of the Board of Deacons to come to the devotional with some music that was meaningful to him or her. He also asked us to bring some scripture that related to the music. The mix of music and scripture that the deacons and the Pastor shared that evening was inspiring and enlightening. I think that the music that was shared gave some interesting insight into each of our spiritual journeys.

I was so inspired by this particular devotional that I decided to compile all the music that we had discussed into a CD mix entitled "Music That Moves the Spirit." Our hope is to use this CD as another way to help the congregation get better acquainted with the members of the Board of Deacons. Can you match the deacon (the Pastor included) with his or her chosen song? We will give the congregation the opportunity to do this by making available short representative samples of each piece of music each member of the Board shared. The samples will be available for listening by the congregation on the church's website and also before and after each worship service in the month of September. Ballots will be available for you to make your guesses. The individual with the most correct answers will be awarded a prize to be announced. In case of a tie, a drawing will be held. Let's have some fun as you try to see how well you know your Board of Deacons.

> *"Let the word of Christ dwell in you richly; teach and admonish*
> *one another in all wisdom; and with gratitude in your hearts*
> *sing psalms, hymns, and spiritual songs to God."*

COL 3:16

May you always feel God's presence in your life!

Lessons from Irene

Bridget Melien

▲ ▲ ▲

FOR THOSE OF YOU THAT DON'T KNOW ME WELL, it's been said that from time to time I'm rule resistant. So when the trucks with the loudspeakers came through the neighborhood on Saturday afternoon calling for mandatory evacuation, I resisted and made the decision to stay at the beach during the storm.

There it was at 9:15 on Sunday morning and I'm glued to the window watching the marsh I overlook like a rubbernecker on a highway. There's no marsh grass visible, the water is rushing in, and the first dumpster goes floating by. I wonder what it's going to look like in another two hours when the tide is fully high. The wind is picking up, and the ocean is just streaming across the road and into the marsh. Wood, debris, a refrigerator, chairs all go by moving fast.

And then I see her, solid and strong, bending but not letting go. And I am amazed and in awe of her. The osprey is sitting on her nest. And although the storm is gaining strength and the water is approaching her platform, she's not letting no, not abandoning her post, not for nothing. I keep checking to see if she is there, and she is, holding tight. And she never moves, never abandons what she knows to be true and strong throughout the storm. I imagine her faith is stronger, stronger than the wind and water, stronger than the dumpster and the debris that couldn't hold on, and stronger than my faith has been at times too. I haven't always been as strong as she is, trusting that God is where my refuge is. I've wavered, perhaps thinking that I could solve whatever struggle I was facing on my own. I've not always held tight, but let go and been separated from my foundation, only to realize after the fact that God is truly what I need to hold on to.

In the midst of the storm, and totally unexpected, I learned that I want to be the osprey.

> *He who dwells in the shelter of the Most High will abide*
> *in the shadow of the Almighty. I will say to the Lord, "My*
> *refuge and my fortress, my God, in whom I trust."*

Ps 91: 1-2

Blessings

Betsy Bascom

I DON'T KNOW ABOUT YOU, but I find this age of 24/7 news and commentary to be exceedingly depressing. There are times when all I want to do is crawl into bed to hide from it. I have found that it is necessary to balance what I listen and watch with reading and meditating on the God. One of the ways I do this is to reflect on all of the blessings the Lord, through his grace and mercy, has bestowed upon me. For the life of me, I cannot fathom why he would be as gracious as he has been to me because I do not honor him with my words and my deeds as I should. Be that as it may, God has graced me and I am exceedingly humbled. Here are a few of the many blessings the Lord has given me, in no particular order:

- His presence in my life and the joy that it brings.
- A strong and loving marriage with God at the center.
- Two wonderful children who have a strong commitment to the family and I hope a growing acceptance of the Lord.
- My dad, a man of great faith and compassion. I am grateful for every minute the Lord has given me with him.
- Strong Christian role models in my life, especially my mom and dad
- My brothers and sisters (in-laws included!), nieces and nephews, aunts, uncles and cousins and the strong heritage of family
- The beauty of the Lyman Farm and all that the Lord has given us as stewards of the land

- My Church family
- My circle of friends from all walks of my life and the joy they bring to me each and every day.
- My health
- The comfort and peace of my home
- My job and the joy of the children
- The promise that each new day brings.
- The beauty of the seasons, the dawn, the twilight-God's creation.
- Our family dog and cat
- The food on my table
- A clear and sound mind (although there are times when I question this!).

As God stated,

> *"I will bless them and the places surrounding my hill. I will send down showers in season; there will be showers of blessing."*

(EZEK 34:26)

I pray that I am worthy of all the blessings that God continues to give to me!

Christmas Gifts
Roger Brewer

The angel said to her [Mary], "And now, you will conceive in your womb and bear a son, and you will name him Jesus. He will be great, and will be called the Son of the Most High, and the Lord God will give to him the throne of his ancestor David. He will reign over the house of Jacob forever, and of his kingdom there will be no end".

Lk 1:31-33 NRSV

SOON WE WILL BE CELEBRATING THE BIRTH OF JESUS, our Lord and Savior.

Whether or not Jesus would be pleased with the way we celebrate his birthday, we enter now the season of Christmas shopping, Christmas songs, nuts, cakes, pies, and candy. We enter the season of Christmas trees, fully decorated with lights and a variety of ornaments. We enter the season of Christmas worship, Christmas prayers, gatherings with family and friends, gift giving, and tales of Santa Claus on rooftops with his reindeer and sleigh. We enter the season of excitement and anticipation.

As a young boy, my primary anticipation and excitement during the Christmas season was with the question of what toys or other similar goodies would I receive as gifts on Christmas morning. Today I am much older and no longer celebrate Christmas as I did when a young boy. Yet, during this special time of the year, I still have that great anticipation and excitement about receiving gifts. However, my anticipation and excitement today involves gifts of a different kind.

Today I get excited about gifts of a spiritual nature, such as the gift of healing from a past hurt or disappointment, the gift of a strengthened and rejuvenated faith in God, the gift of hope restored, the gift of enlightenment on a troubling issue, and other similar gifts that lighten my burden and bring me closer to God.

It has been my practice now for a number of years, during each Christmas season, to hope for the specific spiritual gift or gifts that I feel I need at that particular time. I feel Christmastime is the perfect time to be open to God's gifts. After all, this is the time that we celebrate God's most precious gift to the world, the gift of Jesus and his ministry.

ALMIGHTY GOD, I thank you for my physical, mental and spiritual wellbeing. I thank you for my home, my family, my friends, my relationships, and my daily bread. I thank you for all the blessings you bring into my life. At this time of the year, I thank you especially for the gift of Jesus and the way his powerful ministry operates in my life to uplift me and strengthen me and help me to grow closer to you. I pray at this time for a special gift or two to help me see more clearly and be at peace with how you want me to live my life as opposed to my own personal preferences. I pray also for all of my brothers and sisters around the world, wherever they may be, and whatever life circumstances they may be facing, that they also may receive special gifts, each and everyone, to uplift, strengthen, restore and encourage them, each according to his or her own particular needs. I pray for a special season of healing for all of your children, and that we all may grow closer to you. Amen.

2012

▲▲▲

Receiving Life Gracefully

Michael Satagaj

*"The most important decision we make is whether we
believe that we live in a friendly or hostile universe."*

ALBERT EINSTEIN

STUMBLING ONTO THAT QUOTE in the weeks before Christmas, my
initial thought was that the universe can be ruthlessly hostile, with an abundance of supporting evidence. Before mentioning human on human injustices
and atrocities, we know that we've a tall order just in surviving the natural
elements, even during relatively tranquil periods, and even with modern ame-
nities. My mind next brought me to the several New Testament teachings that
guide us toward 'being in the world, not of it'. It is a recurring commandment
to place your focus in the Lord and only the Lord, a sizeable discipline. It also
suggests an irrelevance to the universe' demeanor, real or perceived, only that
we respond as Christians. The idea though, was not novel to Christ or his followers. I find myself increasingly drawn to the insight of the Old Testament
Book of Ecclesiastes. Solomon bluntly illustrates a fundamental premise that
the world *is and must be* balanced between diametrically opposing energies,
what we might off-handedly label as friendly or hostile. Taking it intimately
further, he proposes that in the end even the virtuous will suffer the same fate
as the less so. He schools us that no one person is immune to temptation or

arrogance or folly, but especially death. Retracing the connection to the New Testament, we find Jesus cautioning against our propensity to glorify our 'works'. He warns against judging our neighbor, against elevating ourselves and against storing up treasures on earth. In each case, the sole answer is reverence of God.

> *"I know that everything God does will endure forever; nothing can be added to it and nothing taken from it. God does it so that men will revere Him,*
>
> ECCL 3:14.*"*

It is now the time of year when many of us take a harder inventory of ourselves, the time of year when we plot to improve ourselves and our circumstances. Rather than committing to an earthly improvement, might we be better served by embracing each moment, or by "just" being, or by "just" allowing? Rather than desiring progress and comfort, might we gain much more by understanding that our creations are temporary? Rather than constantly striving for "solution", might we practice receiving life gracefully, whether in triumph or by trial? Perhaps many occasions call mostly for a smile.

May 2012 find each of you arriving to the inner quiet that is God.

Being Grounded

Karen Bergenholtz

"YOU'RE GROUNDED!"

Ah yes, the dreaded words of a parent, attempting to take you down a notch, restricting access to friends and activities that bring enjoyment. Maybe you escaped such a parenting technique, maybe not. Most have experienced a time-out, or "go to your room" instruction at some point in life.

Remember in Luke, 2:41-52, and the description of Jesus traveling to Jerusalem with his parents for Passover, where Jesus stays behind with Mary and Joseph unaware of his absence for a day? When Mary questions why, Jesus responds, "Why were you searching for me? Didn't you know I had to be in my Father's house?"

One could play out the scene different way—how does a parent respond to seeming precociousness? Would Jesus be expected to sweep the dirt floor of their house? No play dates for a week?

Grounding always carried a negative connotation – punishment for some deed done, or not done. How about looking at it another way. Usually time alone, with distractions of life removed could be used to contemplate your situation, a time to check in with your true self perhaps – being grounded.

Paul and I volunteered to participate in the Living Nativity – the weekend before Christmas. The possibilities were endless of what to do with our time in preparation for December 25. None would have been as meaningful as my meager role as a shepherd. I thought about not washing for a few weeks beforehand, to bring life to my character. Hmm—no. We had a unique experience, sharing a small part of the story that is Christmas, especially being around the young (in age and spirit).

Being part of that rag-tag acting ensemble grounded me – and will remain one of my fondest Christmas memories for years to come. As life sends out the unexpected, I am grateful for the constancy of God's presence, and the life that is the Middlefield Federated Church.

Emmanuel

(God with us)

Being a Christian is Work

Lori Michaud

▲ ▲ ▲

BEING A CHRISTIAN IS NOT EASY. Jesus spent his time on earth embracing the outcasts, the reviled, and the dirty. He spent his time promoting tolerance, love, and acceptance. He took perceptions of society and turned them on their ear. Jesus made a lowly Samaritan the hero of the well-known Good Samaritan parable. He had dinner with the hated tax collector. He pardoned a thief on the cross. Christians are called to be like Christ. It takes work to understand someone who has a different point of view, different backgrounds, and different beliefs.

God speaks to everyone in a unique and personal way. If the Trinity is to be believed in, then we must also recognize that Christians relate to God through the Son, the Jewish tradition relates to God as the Father, and Pagans relate to God as the Spirit. Each aspect is equally important, equally meaningful, and equally valid. If we look past the presentation, we will discover that the information He gives each of us is the same. Be compassionate. Take care of each other. Love is a necessity.

My job as a Christian is to see things from other perspectives, to look at people through the lens of the loving God I know. I strive to learn to accept people for whom and what they are, even if their beliefs are different from mine on the surface. I strive to look deeper to find the similarities. I strive to look deeper to find understanding. I do this so I can be compassionate. So I can take care of others. So I can love by following Christ's example.

Rest in Peace

Paul Bergenholtz

THIS MONTH'S MESSAGE IS DIFFICULT TO WRITE, as we recently lost our fellow deacon and friend, Richard Kennedy. Richard was one of the original members of the Board of Deacons and he served as its first chairman. His special gift was as a teacher and mentor to the children of this church, whom he cherished. We all know that Richard's spirit will live in the hearts of all those who he loved and influenced.

Richard, it was a blessing to be your friend and we will miss you. Rest in peace.

"Train up a child in the way he should go: and when he is old, he will not depart from it."

PROV 22:6(KJV)

Richard Kennedy 1949-2012

We Are All Connected

Sharon Roundtree-Brewer

In the same way, even though we are many individuals, Christ makes
us one body and individuals who are connected to each other.

ROM 12:5 (GWT).

SEVERAL YEARS AGO, MY HUSBAND roger and I started walking each day early in the morning. We started walking primarily for exercise but as time went on our walks became a meditation and devotional for me. I started using the hour we walked together to strengthen my relationship with God. Sometimes Roger and I walk in silence, noticing the sights, signs, and smells of the beautiful earth that God has created and being thankful for all that we have been able to witness. Sometimes we discuss some devotional that we had read or the sermon that the Pastor had preached the previous Sunday. Our discussions about how a particular devotional or sermon relates to us in our spiritual journey also strengthen my relationship with God. However, the latest addition to my walk, something that I have been doing for more than a year now, gives me great pleasure and reinforces one of my most cherished spiritual beliefs.

For more than a year, Roger and I have been waving to every vehicle that we encounter on our walk. We wave to the vehicles moving in both directions. Since we have been walking the same route for years, many people recognize us as their neighbors or that couple that walks, but most of these people do not know us personally. Nearly everyone waves back and some wave rather enthusiastically. I especially love it when toddlers in their car seat laugh and wave. But no matter if the reply is a thumbs-up through the sunroof or a tentative nod of the head, every time someone responds to my wave I feel a real sense of connection. I feel God's love.

Paul says, "Christ makes us one body and individuals who are connected to each other." Over the past several months, many of the people who respond to my wave have confirmed this connection. On more than one occasion several people have stopped their cars to tell Roger and me how much they appreciated being acknowledged, how our wave to them made their day, or picked them up. A few people in the grocery store or pharmacy have also approached us with the question, "Are you the couple who walks every morning?" When we say we are, they tell us how much our wave meant to them as they drove to their destination that day. For me, this means that I am not the only one who feels this connection and God's love.

My prayer is that we all come to understand and believe that we are truly connected. If we believe this and honor this connection in the depths of our hearts, we will honor and take care of each other.

If one part of the body suffers, all the other parts share its suffering.
If one part is praised, all the others share in its happiness.

1 Cor 12:26 (NRSV)

May you always feel God's presence in your life.

In the Garden

Bridget Melien

"Gardens bring us into contact with the cycles and irrefutable
laws of nature, teaching us indelible lessons about ourselves and
about the messy, difficult, and beautiful processes of living."

— CAIT JOHNSON IN *EARTH, WATER, FIRE, AND AIR*

THE SUN PEEPS UP OVER THE HORIZON, the birds have long been
up singing their morning songs. No voices, no machines, just the steady move-
ments of prayer, bending, tucking a seedling into it's new home, removing a
weed or two and being in quiet time with God.

I think God knit this into me long before I was born as it is the place
I am truly most at peace with myself and the world. I embrace the sense
of "groundedness" literally and have never been very far away from the dirt
throughout my life. This time and space embodies who I am at my core and
embraces all I hope to be on my life journey.

It is God's story of life for me all contained in one place. Imagination
of new life, turning the cold soil in the spring, starting seedlings under the
lights in February, waiting to set them into the warming earth, nurturing and
watching God's magic right under my fingertips. Then comes the sharing
with friends and family, rejoicing in the bounty God has provided and finally
putting it to bed for a long winters sleep. The cycle, over and over, always sure

that it will come again. There is comfort in the knowing that it has come before me, and is a shared experience of humankind, and that there's ever present hope it will go on and on. And that God has provided it for all of us freely.

Enjoy your season gardeners, new and old. May you find joy, peace and God's blessings there.

MFC Evening Bible Study
Betsy Bascom

O Lord, you have searched me. And you know me.
You know when I sit and when I rise;
you perceive my thoughts from afar.
You discern my going out and my lying down;
you are familiar with all my ways.
Before a word is on my tongue
you know it completely, O Lord.

Ps 139: 1-4

ABOUT EIGHT YEARS AGO I was asked to participate in *Unwrapping Our Gifts*, the wonderful course the church has run several times now. Participants discover through the course the gifts given to them by God and are then encouraged to bring these gifts to fruition. I discovered that I had a great desire to organize an evening Bible Study. I wanted to read and talk about the Word of God with others in our faith community; reading it on my own was no longer enough. So far our group has studied the books of Genesis, Esther and Ruth, Jeremiah, Luke, John, Acts and have just concluded the Psalms' We are a congenial group, engaging in thought provoking conversations that lead in many directions. I often come home after one of our sessions feeling invigorated. There is so much that I do not know about the Scriptures, but the Bible

Study is certainly helping me to learn and apply God's teaching to my life. One of the perks of being in the group is choosing the study for the following year. We have been alternating between the Old and New Testaments, and so next year we will venture back into the New Testament when we study the book of Romans. There is no leader in our group. The study guides we use have been written to help the participants capture the essence of each book through readings about key passages. Following each reading are questions for reflection, which we use to get the discussion going' Sometimes we follow these questions closely, other times the Holy Spirit leads us in an entirely different direction. No matter what, it is always lively, interesting and a true learning experience. And so I invite you to watch the weekly bulletin and *Red Doors* in the fall for an announcement about our next study. I hope you will join us and become part of our wonderful group!

Prayer

Roger Brewer

*"Answer me when I call, O God of my right! You gave me room
when I was in distress. Be gracious to me, and hear my prayer."*

Ps 4:1

I DON'T KNOW ABOUT YOU, but sometimes when I pray I pray for a
lot of things.

And sometimes I really get it going. I give thanks for all of my blessings,
specifically naming many of them such as my physical health, my material
possessions, my relationships with others, and the health and welfare of love
ones, family and friends. I pray for my church and my church family. I pray
for forgiveness of my sins. I pray for those who are hungry. I pray for the poor
and victims of war and other violence. I pray for the healing of specific people
on my mind. I pray for people known to me to be struggling with different
issues. I pray for people who appear to be doing just fine. I pray for reconciliation and peace on earth. I go on and on and on.

It is no surprise to you, I'm sure, that God does not answer all of my
prayers in the way I would like God to answer them. One might say, and I
would agree, that if God grants only some of my petitions, then what a blessing that is.

I open my eyes and realize today that there is a great benefit to me in my praying in addition to the granting of any of my petitions. Now don't get wrong. I would prefer that my petitions be granted. However, when they are not granted, there is nevertheless a great benefit to me.

My praying alone puts me in a closer relationship with God. It strengthens me on the inside. It increases my faith, courage and perseverance. It helps me with discernment and sustains me in ways too many to name them.

I give thanks for the blessings of prayer.

ALMIGHTY GOD, I pray for me. I pray for others as well, including all of your children. I pray that we might always keep our lines of communications with you open and clear, filled with integrity, honesty and love. May we always feel your mighty presence in our lives. And may we never feel alone. Amen.

SEPTEMBER 1

"Grasshopper, Snatch the Pebble from My Hand"

Michael Satagaj

IN THE SPIRIT OF THE PENDING SCHOOL YEAR:

After being interviewed by the school administration, the teaching prospect said, "Let me see if I've got this right: You want me to go into that room with all those kids, correct their disruptive behavior, observe them for signs of abuse, monitor their dress habits, censor their T-shirt messages, and instill in them a love for learning. You want me to check their backpacks for weapons, wage war on drugs and sexually transmitted diseases, and raise their sense of self-esteem and personal pride.

You want me to check their heads for lice, recognize signs of antisocial behavior, and make sure that they all pass the state exams. You want me to provide them with an equal education regardless of their handicaps, and communicate regularly with their parents by e-mail, telephone, newsletter, and report card.

You want me to do all this with a piece of chalk, a blackboard, a bulletin board, a few books, a big smile, and a starting salary that qualifies me for food stamps. You want me to do all this, and then you tell me.............. I CAN'T PRAY?"

Though the tools of the trade and the salary considerations are a little outdated, the message certainly bears an ironic relevance. And not just to the certified, professional teachers among us. In every capacity that we entertain, all of us mentor and teach or demonstrate something to someone else. Make no mistake, in the simplest of exchanges, when you offer patience, when you offer humility, when you offer honesty and graciousness, you are teaching. So, what is at the core of the knowledge that you share?

"Trust in the Lord with all your heart and lean
not on your own understanding."

PROV 3:5

Within the study bible that I own, the Book of Proverbs, dedicated to obtaining and sharing wisdom, is prefaced with the following: Knowledge is good, but there is a vast difference between *knowledge* (having the facts) and *wisdom* (applying those facts to life). We may amass knowledge, but without wisdom, our knowledge is useless. We must learn how to live out what we know.

We should share knowledge with each other. And we should pray about that knowledge. And we should never stop seeking His wisdom.

Worry (I)

Barb Carlin

Who of you by worrying can add a single hour to your life?
Therefore, do not worry about tomorrow, for tomorrow will
worry about itself. Each day has enough trouble of its own.

MT 6:27, 34

BOTH MY MOTHER AND MY MOTHER-IN-LAW WERE THE BEST of Christian women. They attended church regularly, prayed daily and handed down to us kids the greatest of Christian values. My mother was probably the queen of "what will be, will be", while my mother-in-law tended to be overly concerned about everything from A to Z. In Matthew 6:25-34 Jesus gives us a wonderful lesson about worrying.

As Bob and I are reaching a new and exciting point in our lives, I find a lot of 'worrys' creeping in. After all, retirement is a real life change for all of us. No longer will I be able to look up at the doorframe in front of my desk and see a sign that tells me "Don't Let Them Steal Your Peace". (I'll miss that sign, but not the reason it is there). I decided that once again I needed to look to the bible to get me through another stage of my life. Who thought there would be so many stages?

As it turns out, there are numerous places in the bible that caution us about worry and anxiety. Philippians 4:6 reminds us to first pray concerning everything. "Do not be anxious about anything, but in everything, by prayer and petition, with thanksgiving, present your requests to God".

Or how about 1 Peter 5:6-7? "Humble yourself, therefore, under God's mighty hand that He might lift you up in due time. Cast all your anxiety on Him because He cares for you". I like the "due time" part of this lesson, as I have learned over the years that just because God doesn't answer me today or tomorrow does not mean that he hasn't heard my prayer. God is always on a different timetable than I am. He may not answers your prayers in the way you are expecting or when you want them answered, but be assured that He has heard you and will answer in His time.

And lastly, I also know that God helps those who help themselves. If I truly want peace and less anxiety in my life, I need to do my part to keep myself out of stressful situations as much as possible. I need to think positively and do whatever I can to help God help me.

Joyce Meyer said, "Worry is the opposite of Faith". Let's all keep the faith! God's Grace to All.

For All the Saints

Karen Bergenholtz

▲ ▲ ▲

AS WE PUT OUR GARDENS TO BED, with lingering warm days, thoughts turn to November and thanks giving. My thanks begin with the saints who have touched my life since moving to Middlefield. These are not the saints of my childhood, statues with haloes, but living beings here in our midst, folks who do the work to bring a Living Christ to our community and the world.

Many years ago during a brief conversation in the pews following the postlude, D.A., Paul and I chatted about how the word "love" is spoken so easily. D.A. remarked that there needed to be a show of love, not just words. Which brings me back to my remembrances of certain individuals who demonstrated love in our midst by their actions and dedication to their faith and community. I'm sure there are blatant omissions and please forgive me, but indulge me by sharing a prayer for these lives:

D.A.—for the twinkle in her eye and the force of her voice
D.R.—for his commitment to community
P.H. and E.H.—welcoming spirits
J.G.—he could build anything, faithful and giving
C.C.—for his quiet nature and faith
E.L.—for inviting me to Women's Fellowship
M.C.—her zest
R.K.—the man, his commitment to young lives

D.C. and H.C.—inseparable
G.R.—unfailing
L.G.—she could burn the candle at both ends successfully
B.P.—her faith and love of music
T.H.—the wind beneath B's wings
B.S.—courage and love
I.H.—for love of laughter and friendship with quiet faith
R.R.—tick, tock, the clock man
H.G.—for friendship
S.H.—who taught me how to read the bible, seeing it in new ways
G.L.—our gentle spirit, loving and generous
A.M. and J.M.—energy!!!!
B.P.—gracious and full of faith
R.P.—dedicated
E.T.—welcomed us, encouraging Paul in attending the men's Palm
Sunday service
R.W.—confident and encouraging in faith

Surely there are others, and perhaps these folks have not affected you personally, but I believe there are saints in your life as well. Thanks be to God! "For all the saints, who from their labours rest, Who Thee by faith before the world confessed, Thy Name, O Jesus, be forever blessed. Alleluia, Alleluia!"

> *"It was he who gave some to be apostles, some to be prophets,*
> *some to be evangelists, and some to be pastors and teachers, to*
> *prepare God's people for the works of service, so that the body*
> *of Christ may be built up until we all reach unity in the faith*
> *and in the knowledge of the Son of God and become mature,*
> *attaining to the whole measure of the fullness of Christ".*

FROM EPH 4:11

We all have the ability to be a saint, to work for Christ in the world. Our world can be overwhelming, but consider the words from Mother Teresa, "God does not command that we do great things, only little things with great love".

DECEMBER 1

Merry Christmas
Paul Bergenholtz

HAVE A MERRY CHRISTMAS. It is easy phrase to say, but difficult to do. Studies have shown that for many people Christmas can be and probably is the most stressful time of the year.

The first signs of stress occur when dealing with the onslaught of advertisements from retailers suggesting subtly and not so subtlety that unless we find the perfect gift for our loved ones, Christmas will be "a bust." Some people, mostly women, may actually enjoy shopping for that special gift, but if you are a guy ... well most of us are just clueless when it comes to gift shopping. And a little suggestion for the guys, December 24th is not the best day to go shopping at the mall after you have procrastinated for weeks. Talk about stress!

However, the greatest type of stress is the family dynamic stress that comes from strained relations, loneliness due to the passing of a loved one, or not being able to be with family due to distance or competing obligations of others. This type of stress is probably most prevalent during the holidays for many people and for us as well.

As we journey through the Season of Advent, let our stress be relieved by reminding ourselves that we should be celebrating the birth of our Lord and Savior, Jesus Christ and how his birth changed our lives and our world. The description of events leading up to Jesus' birth is found in Matthew 1: 18 – 23:

This is how the birth of Jesus Christ came about: His mother Mary was pledged to be married to Joseph, but before they came together, she was found to be with child through the Holy Spirit. Because Joseph her husband was a righteous man and did not want to expose her to public disgrace, he had in mind to divorce her quietly.

But after he had consider this, an angel of the Lord appeared to him in a dream and said, "Joseph son of David, do not be afraid to take Mary home as your wife, because what is conceived in her is from the Holy Spirit. She will give birth to a son, and you are to give him the name Jesus, because he will save his people from their sins.

All this took place to fulfill what the Lord had said through the prophet: "The virgin will be with child and will give birth to a son, and they will call him Immanuel" – which means, "God with us." NIV

Let God be with all of us during this holiday season.

Merry Christmas.

2013
▲▲▲

Experiencing God in the Silence

Roger Brewer

I LOOK BACK OVER THE YEAR 2012 and make a list of the people, occurrences and developments in my life that have impacted me in my spiritual growth and development in a significant way. I study the list to see if I can discern any trends of the year or appreciate more deeply how God may be working in my life. My reflection on the list continues. But one thing that impresses me so far is that during the latter part of 2012 I began to focus on how God speaks to me in the silence.

For sure I find myself constantly speaking to God in prayer. I'm constantly asking God for forgiveness. I'm constantly expressing my gratitude and appreciation for the blessings in my life. I'm constantly petitioning God for help in my anxieties and concerns. But communication with God is a two-way street. To what extent do I pay attention when God speaks to me?

I believe I make a good effort to hear God when God speaks to me through other people, through nature, through scripture, and through other external occurrences. However, I do not believe I have done enough in the recent past to hear or experience God in the silence.

"Be still, and know that I am God!"

PSALM 46:10

"For God alone my soul waits in silence, for my hope is from [God]."

Ps 62:5

The silence in which I experience or hear God is not the same as the absence of external noise. The silence I speak of is the suspension of that chain of thoughts that runs continuously through the mind. Can you go to that state of existence where conscious thoughts in your mind are temporarily suspended, even if only for a short period of time, even a brief moment? Perhaps you can experience a series of such moments during a single meditation session.

But how, you might ask, does God speak to us in the silence? After all, silence is silence. My response is that I don't know, but I do know it happens. Experiencing or hearing God in the silence does not mean I see visions or hear audible voices from above. It does not mean I encounter burning bushes that are not consumed or experience other incidents of an extraordinary kind. But something does happen to me that is quite magnificent.

As I continue my practice of quieting the mind, I become filled more fully with love for my brothers and sisters around the world. I become less judgmental and fearful of others. I have less anxiety in my life. I become more appreciative of the many blessings that I have in my life right now. I have greater insight into what's going on in my personal life and in the wider world in which I live. I feel closer to God and more confident that God is indeed with me always.

ALMIGHTY GOD, I pray for me and all of my brothers and sisters throughout the world, wherever they may be, whoever they may be, and in whatever circumstances they may find themselves. May we all be open to receive your spirit and your powerful love by whatever avenue you have made available to us. Be with us and guide us with your love and comfort throughout this year and thereafter forevermore. Amen.

Honeybees

Betsy Bascom

In the beginning was the Word, and the Word was with God, and the Word was God. He was with God in the beginning. Through him all things were made; without him nothing was made that has been made.

JN 1:1-3

MY HUSBAND ACQUIRED A NEW HOBBY over the last couple of years: beekeeping. It has been a learning curve for all of us, but most especially for our son Jack who has been drafted on numerous occasions to assist Bob in transferring the new bees he has bought to the hives. My daughter Maggie and I have wisely chosen to be spectators and enjoy being entertained from the deck during these occasions.

I will say that I have become more accustomed to the bees with the passing of time. The honeybees have become a part of our daily existence. I will be sitting on the deck in the summer enjoying my morning devotions or the papers when I will look up and there will be a bee nearby, usually sitting quietly. Resting perhaps? I am always amazed at the utter perfection of God's creation in the honeybee. They are beautiful, small with a soft covering of brown and yellow fur. The structure of a hive is amazing in its organization from the queen to the workers to the drones.

I find it difficult to comprehend that such creatures evolved by chance. When I think about all they do and how instrumental they are to our very existence, I am certain God, our Creator, was the creator of the honeybee as well. Beginning on the very first warm days, the hives spring to life following the long winter's rest. I watch the bees dart in and out of the hive, never seeming to tire. Did you know that bees travel up to a mile and a half to gather nectar and pollen to bring back to the hive? In fact, I have often wondered if I am seeing some of Bob's bees in the gardens at John Lyman School as I travel out to the portable classrooms. Most of our food sources would not exist without bees, since pollination is necessary in the growing of fruits and vegetables. The honey the bees make never spoils and is widely believed to be a homeopathic remedy for many of our physical ailments. God, in his infinite wisdom, created the honeybee to live in harmony with man and to provide sustenance for him.

For by him all things were created; things in heaven and on earth,
visible and invisible… all things were created by him and for him.

Col 1: 1

How many are your works, O Lord! In wisdom you
made them all: the earth is full of your creatures.

Ps 104:24

God's Love

Sharon Roundtree-Brewer

*Let us think of ways to motivate one another to acts of love
and good works. And let us not neglect our meeting together,
as some people do, but encourage one another . . .*

HEB 10:24-25 (NLT)

"CAN I BE A CHRISTIAN WITHOUT GOING TO CHURCH?" was the title of the unit for one of our recent confirmation class sessions and we, the youth and mentors, participated in activities designed to help us wrestle with this question. For some, this might be an easy question to answer. For others, it is far more complicated and might lead to more questions such as "What is a Christian?" and "What do we mean by church?" and, well, you get the idea. These questions are much too complex to tackle in this space, so I'll leave that to another time. But the question *"Can I Be a Christian Without Going to Church?"* did move me to reflect again on my personal reasons for going to church or attending Sunday morning worship.

Sunday morning worship is a special experience for me. It is an experience of being in community with like-minded people. It is an experience of connecting with people on a deeply spiritual and personal level. It is an experience of love. I experience God's love and God's spirit on Sunday morning at church in a way that I am unable to experience at any other time or in any other place.

The way in which I experience God's love in Sunday worship varies from Sunday to Sunday, but it is always a joyous and moving experience. I feel God's love when someone shares with me a particular joy in her life that happened that week and we both thank God for that blessing. I experience God's love when someone shares a particular hurt with me and we hug and ask God for patience and strength. I experience God's love when we gather around a prayer shawl, each of us reaching to touch the shawl or another's shoulder, to fill that shawl with our love and healing energy. I feel God's love when our dedicated choir 'nails' a particular anthem so perfectly that the congregation bursts into applause or shouts of amen. I feel God's love when we share our joys and concerns with each other. I feel God's love in the smiles of the children in the church. And I feel God's love in the special way that our pastor connects with the congregation. The many ways in which I feel God's love are far too numerous to recount here, but I never fail to feel that love on Sunday morning at church.

May you experience God's love each Sunday that you attend worship. May God's love nourish and strengthen you in the ways that you need it. And may God's love help all of us to motivate each other to acts of love and good works.

Fear

Bridget Melien

*For I am the Lord, your God, who takes hold of your right
hand and says to you, Do not fear; I will help you.*

ISA 41:13

HAVE YOU EVER FOUND YOURSELF IN THIS SITUATION? A big
change in your life is on the horizon, perhaps moving your family, a career
or job change, or starting or ending a relationship? You agonize over it, make
a pros and cons list, pray over it? The day comes, you make the big decision
finally and move forward. A few weeks later it occurs to you, "Why did I wait
so long? Why was I so afraid?"

What is it about change that makes us fearful? Is it the unknown? The
fear that we might fail at the new endeavor? The comfort of the familiar? And
what IS IT about fear, real or otherwise, anyway?

I've been in this situation countless times and each time it reminds me of
something I discovered in my twenties. I wasn't seeking it, at the time I just
recall it happening. I've never been a great sleeper, and the discovery grew
out of that as I remember. Each night I began taking out my fears, examin-
ing them and then embracing them. Yes, I am sure a sleep expert would tell
me this was the worst thing ever. But what happened over time was that the
process of embracing the fear put it in perspective, and it was no longer scary.

The crazy thing about this experience is that now I forget about it and go for long periods where fear and change are scary.

What's the point of all of this? In my most recent re-discovery, I think I now recognize that this was God guiding and protecting me all those years ago when I had this experience for the first time. He knows me so intimately that He provided me with exactly what I needed, though I did not recognize it at the time. Perhaps the in-between times were when I wasn't listening or being open in my heart for His grace.

I pray daily now that I can listen for His voice, open my heart to His grace and accept that He truly knows exactly what I need, now and always.

Get on the Bus?

Karen Bergenholtz

▲ ▲ ▲

SEVERAL NIGHTS AGO I DREAMED I was on a school bus with the bus driver, another adult, and two children. The driver and the other adult got off the bus with one child, leaving me with the other child. When they were out of sight the bus began rolling and I could not find the emergency braking system. We were rolling down a winding, sloping road, with an embankment on the right, and I needed to alternate focus on steering and looking for the braking system. We finally coasted to a stop when the downhill momentum ended. Someone climbed on to the bus and there it was – a small button in front of the steering column that engaged the brake. So how would you interpret this? Is this dream telling me I'm not in control, or perhaps a solution is right in front of me, or I'm trying to deal with more than I should be....

One of the next day's worship service lessons was John 21:1-14, where the disciples are trying to fish without result, until "the disciple whom Jesus loved" recognized Christ as the person on the shore who was instructing them. Jesus had instructed the fisherman (disciples) to throw the net on the right side of the boat. Somehow I was stuck on verse 6, "they were unable to haul the net in because of the large number of fish." What? Jesus tells them what to do, but the abundance of their catch is too great; the recognition of Christ is what brings them success. Still I was stuck on how the abundance that Christ provided was overwhelming, more than they could handle. Should we imagine Christ standing on shore chuckling at the disciples trying to haul all those fish into their boat? Surely there might have been provided only enough for them to handle immediately. Until Christ is recognized, they are unable to handle the abundance.

A line from the hymn, "How Great Thou Art" comes to mind: "And when I think that God, his son not sparing Sent him to die, I scarce can take it in." It is overwhelming —God cares for us that much. There is abundant Grace available to us.

From the Old Testament, Deuteronomy 8:16-18, "He gave you manna to eat in the desert, something your fathers had never known, to humble and to test you so that in the end it might go well with you. You may say to yourself, "My power and the strength of my hands have produced this wealth for me. But remember the Lord your God, for it is he who gives you the ability to produce wealth, and so confirms his covenant, which he swore to your forefathers, as it is today."

On that particular Sunday the men's choir from Teen Challenge visited, with several sharing testimony of the difficulties in their lives and of the healing they find through Christ. One of the men shared a realization that God is not done with him yet. Another individual shared his story, of no matter how successful, he never felt good enough, how his attempt at filling this emptiness lead him down a treacherous road.

I ask you to pray with me, for me, for anyone who needs to recognize the help that comes through God.

"All This Time, the River Flows, Endlessly, to The Sea"—Sting

Lori Michaud

▲ ▲ ▲

MOVING WATER SCULPTS THE EARTH. We see it in the mountain ranges. We see it on the coastlines. We see it in the river valleys. When my family went to Acadia National Park and stood on the top of Cadillac Mountain we were able to see the scars that the glaciers left behind. Meigs Point is a depository of boulders pushed along by those glaciers. The entire northeast coastline was altered by tidal surges during hurricane Sandy. The Grand Canyon was carved by the Colorado River. What I am saying is this: Moving water is powerful.

Keep that in mind while you read this next thing:

> *He who believes in Me, as the Scripture has said, out of his heart will flow rivers of living water.*

JN 7:38

Rivers + living water = change. We who have chosen to believe are going to be changed. We will be altered in fairly unpredictable ways. Our personal lives are full of changes: First day of school, graduation from high school, living on our own, marriage, becoming parents, the loss of a parent. Each transition requires adjustment. We learn and grow. We develop new appreciation for what these things are. Then, just when we are comfortable, another transition! Sometimes it's a gradual change, like the Grand Canyon. Sometimes it's a sudden change, like hurricane Sandy. While each experience has an impact on our lives that alters us forever, we learn and grow from that experience. Our hearts can be softened and our minds can be opened. Scripture will have new meaning to us. God will show himself in different ways—or maybe he is showing himself in the same way and we haven't been able to see him clearly until now.

But that's not all. The second part is this: We who chose to believe are going to become instruments of change in this world. We are to speak out against injustice. We are to show mercy and compassion for each other. We are to be those ever present, ever moving, living waters that will bring about real, lasting, and peaceful change. It will not always be comfortable, and we may not agree on the best way to serve God in this capacity, but we are called to action. We are to be the change.

When an event occurs that shakes our faith in the church, the government, or our society may we continue believing in the river that flows. My prayer is that we always feel God's powerful presence working in us to shape us into the persons we ought to be, and through us to sculpt the world into a more loving and socially just place.

The Accuser

Michael Satagaj

*And I heard a loud voice in heaven saying, Now is come
salvation, and strength, and the kingdom of our God, and
the power of his Christ: for the accuser of our brethren is cast
down, which accused them before our God day and night.*

REV 12:10

THINK OF THE DIFFERENT SINS that humans are capable of, murder, rape, or assault among the most egregious. The sins of theft, exploitation and adultery perhaps less so. How about vices like envy or greed or sloth? While we like to think that we are above the commission of such behavior or thought, the truth is that we are all guilty. Of the many names in the Bible for Satan (Abaddon (Destruction), Adversary, Angel of Light, Angel of the Bottomless Pit, Antichrist, Apollyon (Destroyer), Beast, Beelzebub, Belial, Devil, Dragon, Enemy, Evil One, Father of Lies, Ruler of Darkness, Ruler of this World, Satan, Serpent of Old, Tempter, Thief, and Wicked One to name a few) it is the Deceiver or the Accuser that most commonly trips us.

Satan distinctly appears three times in the Bible. He first appeared in Genesis, then in Job, and finally in Matthew 4 to Jesus when he brought him to the temple mount. All three times he appeared for the purpose of accusing. In Genesis he came to accuse God to man. In Job he came to accuse man to

God. The Devil is trying to get man to treat God unjustly, and he is trying to get God to treat man unjustly. The third time he came to accuse the God-Man. His entire system is accusation.

The great work of Satan is to disrupt justice. The way he disrupts justice is by accusing. This causes people to judge others based on the accusation, not on the reality.

The Devil is accusing. Right now he is accusing and trying to get us to believe things that are not true. He is attempting to disrupt the entire order of justice on the face of the earth by causing people to be accused of things falsely and being wrongly judged by others (Hyles).

Think on this when you charge your neighbor.

When you charge them with transgression against you or against God or against humanity.

When you charge them with greed or apathy or intolerance or ignorance. Or with sloth or weakness.

When you charge them with being less than you.

The entire 14th chapter in Paul's Letter to the Romans is devoted to teaching you that they too may be acting in God's name and for God's justice.

What Took You So Long?

Paul Bergenholtz

MY HIGH SCHOOL ENGLISH TEACHER once stated that a classmate had read the Bible from beginning to end simply as a literary work. I was impressed by this persons' accomplishment, but I was also surprised about the individual in question, as I did not believe she was particularly religious. This was a bit judgmental on my part, but I have to believe that she got more from the Bible than just a "good read."

Over 40 years later, I have followed the lead of my former classmate and am now on my own journey through the Bible starting with "In the beginning" through to the "Amen." However, my goal is not to simply state that I have read the entire Bible. My goal is to gain wisdom and guidance.

As I write this, I have just finished reading Proverbs, which contain many "wise sayings." Some passages are stern admonitions, while others are uplifting and insightful that still speaks to today's reader. Just imagine if we all followed just one "timeless" example of wisdom found in Proverbs 15:1 … what a better world it would be:

A soft answer turns away wrath, but a harsh word stirs up anger.

PROV 15:1

Although the books of the Bible were written centuries ago, the messages found in them are as relevant today as they were in biblical times. Times may have changed, but the human condition is the same. We are overly concerned about possessions; we fear the unknown and we ignore God's guidance. Acknowledging these truths about ourselves, we should reflect on the message found in Proverbs 3:5-6:

> *Trust in the Lord with all your heart, and do not rely*
> *on your own insight. In all your ways acknowledge*
> *him, and he will make straight your paths.*

Prov 3:5-6

The Bible is a gift from God. Let us give thanks for His gift and use it as our Lord would have intended.

Sunrise and Sunset

Elisabeth Kennedy

Morning has broken, like the first morning.
Blackbird has spoken, like the first bird.
Praise for the singing, praise for the morning,
Praise for them springing fresh from the Word.

Sweet the rain's new fall, sunlight from heaven.
Like the first dewfall, on the first grass.
Praise for the sweetness of the wet garden,
Sprung in completeness where His feet pass.

Mine is the sunlight, mine is the morning.
Born of the one light Eden saw play.
Praise with elation, praise every morning;
God's recreation of the new day.

Morning has broken, like the first morning.
Blackbird has spoken, like the first bird.
Praise for the singing, praise for the morning,
Praise for them springing fresh from the Word.
Songwriter: Stevens, Mark

EVERY YEAR I SPEND TIME IN MAINE—Peaks Island —one of my favorite places in the world. For me, it is a time of rest and renewal, rising early to watch the sunrise, spending hours searching for sea glass, walking, biking, enjoying family, and watching the sunset. On Peaks, the sun rises out of the open sea and sets over Portland. The sun's reflection on the sea accentuates the beauty of the sunrise and sunset. Although both are often spectacular, I prefer the sunrise, perhaps because of the promise of the new day.

As I watched sunrises and sunsets this week, I considered how the sun reflects God's light in our lives. Like the sun, God's presence is constant, although we don't always see it. On clear days, the sunrise is so bright it is difficult to look at, but leaves an orange path of light through the water, almost pulling or leading us to its light. On cloudy days, the sunlight creates prisms of color and light across the sky and sea – a painter's palate of color and light that seems to enfold us into it. Likewise, I have felt God's presence and light in similar ways during different times of my life. Sometimes His presence has been a bright path leading me to Him or His purpose for my life; and through the clouds of trials or troubles, as layers of soft light or comfort that have enfolded me in His grace. In times when I may not feel or see His presence, I am always reassured that, as with the sun, He is always there.

I thank God for His presence in my life and I pray you feel His presence in yours as well. Praise God for the absolute majesty of His creation, from soaring mountains to beautiful seas, from birds that awaken us to the rising of the sun, to family and friends who are also reflections of His love. I pray that God surrounds you as well with powerful, motivating light in good times, gentle light and soft colors of His grace in difficult days, and a constant awareness of His presence, light and love.

Building

Lori Michaud

"With the help of the Holy Spirit, our Mission is to build and
strengthen relationships with God, one another, and our world."

BUILDING IS EASIER WHEN WE HAVE THE RIGHT TOOLS for
the job. Compassion, Consideration, Respect, Vulnerability and Forgiveness
are five key items to keep in our toolbox when it comes to building and
strengthening relationships. It's not enough to have them, though. We have to
use all of them liberally and with wild abandon.

Listening to someone with a compassionate ear makes the speaker feel
loved, valued, and cared for. Simply taking the time to give them your full attention and empathy improves their outlook. You don't even have to have any
answers to whatever is bothering them.

Consideration validates people. Random acts of kindness, mission work,
or simply smiling at a stranger can make someone who is feeling invisible feel
seen and appreciated. Don't forget about those closest to you! Those relationships benefit greatly from unexpected signs of consideration. Something as
simple as holding the door open or offering a drink shows that you are thinking about someone else and their needs.

Respecting one another allows us to debate differing ideals without in-
sulting or defaming each other's character. When we can tackle the difficult
issues, when we can examine our differences with respect, we will create a
stronger bond.

Vulnerability is scary because personal risk is involved. This is where we share our true selves. We need to open ourselves up to the possibility of being disappointed and hurt. We need to trust that we will receive compassion, consideration, and respect. When we can allow ourselves to be vulnerable our relationships will have the opportunity to deepen and be more meaningful than ever before.

Forgiveness allows us to continue when we are let down or hurt in a relationship. Forgiving keeps your heart open, while being forgiven gives us the chance to try again. We are human. Mistakes will be made. We need to forgive each other and ourselves for our shortcomings.

May the Holy Spirit guide us as we grow more proficient with these tools. May our hearts remain open and be filled with forgiveness when human interactions disappoint us. May we experience new depth in our relationships with God, the world, and each other.

God Directs

Valerie Faiella

"You may make your plans, but God directs your actions."

Prov 16:9 (TEV)

PERHAPS YOU CAN IDENTIFY with the following story. BANG! The starter's pistol went off and away I ran on a day filled with a check-off list of ever-important things that I just "had" to do. The morning was progressing nicely - items were being checked off and I was "on schedule". That is, until I hit a store and spotted an acquaintance that I hadn't seen in quite a while. You would think that I would have stopped for a "quick hello". (That would be the polite thing to do.) But, I'm ashamed to admit that I didn't. Instead, I made a quick turn down the aisle in hopes of not getting sidetracked with small talk. There was no time for idle chitchat on this list. That would, of course, throw off the *ever-important race* against time to get the *ever-important list* done. As "luck" would have it, several aisles later, there she was again. About-face I turned quickly to get to another area of the store. I quickly re-did my list in my mind and would come back to that area later. That's when I "heard" it. Not out loud – but that still small voice. "Go back and talk with her". My initial response was "Really God? You *know* how much I have to do. I really don't know her that well and if I stop to talk I may not get this list done." . . . Silence! I took a deep breath and asked "What about the list?" . . .

Silence! SO, I did what an "obedient Christian" would do and I followed directions. I went back to the last aisle I'd seen her and . . . she wasn't there. Oh well, I made the attempt – now I was back on track. That is until I rounded that aisle and there she was. I said "hi" and we talked about superficial things for a bit and then she said "I really needed to talk with someone today. I have a lot going on and I just needed someone that I could confide in and would take the time to listen."

See, there isn't any such thing as "luck". I really believe in divine intervention. There were so many places I could have been at that moment and I wasn't. The store was huge, so I really didn't need to keep "bumping" into her. To this day, I have absolutely NO recollection of what was *so* important on that list. I do recall the gratitude to God for having me right where I needed to be. Maybe she benefited too, but I was reminded of several things. It's good to have plans. It's even better (and generally more efficient) to include God in those plans *and* to be open to when those plans are being re-directed. I wasn't at first. I was almost resentful that "my" priorities weren't being considered. Take time for people – you never know who God will put in your path.

The Merry in Christmas

Michael Satagaj

AT THE TIME OF THIS WRITING it has been an exceptionally busy week. From a couple of evening work engagements, to a pair of hockey games, to the regular tutoring session, to celebrating my eldest daughter's birthday, the activity has flowed. Yet, I have somehow been blessed to experience and recognize distinct special moments with various individuals throughout all of it. And while I hope that each of you can find such moments of quiet or relief or joy or fellowship during the bustle of the season, all I can offer is some encouragement and a bit of humor. So...

> *Seems an elderly lady was well known for her faith and for her boldness in talking about it. She would stand on her front porch and shout "PRAISE THE LORD!"*
>
> *Next door to her lived an atheist who would get so angry at her proclamations he would shout, "There ain't no Lord!"*
>
> *Year after year they antagonized and answered each other.*
>
> *Hard times set in on the elderly lady, and she prayed for GOD to send her some assistance. She stood on her porch and shouted, "PRAISE THE LORD. GOD I NEED FOOD!! I AM HAVING A HARD TIME. PLEASE LORD, SEND ME SOME GROCERIES."*
>
> *The next morning the lady went out on her porch and noted a large bag of groceries and shouted, "PRAISE THE LORD."*

The neighbor jumped from behind a bush and said, "Aha! I told you there was no Lord. I bought those groceries, God didn't."

The lady started jumping up and down and clapping her hands and said, "PRAISE THE LORD. He not only sent me groceries, but He made the devil pay for them. Praise the Lord!"

May you get the best of the devil today. Peace, gratitude and some moments of laughter to all of you this Christmas season.

2014

▲▲▲

Letting Go
Roger Brewer

AS I HAVE SHARED WITH YOU BEFORE on this page, the beginning of a new year is an exciting time for me. Each year as we approach or begin the new year, I like to take inventory of the various things going on in my life. I examine events and occurrences of the past year to see if I can discern patterns, to see if I can recognize messages from on high, to see what changes, if any, I need to make in my life. I ask myself if I need to let go of places, people, foods, thoughts or habits that may be holding me back or harming me in some other way. I set goals and develop plans or strategies to take me where I feel I need to go.

This year I find myself doing the usual annual self-evaluation. However, for the first time, I am struggling with whether I should give up on a lifetime dream to which I have devoted tremendous time and effort over the years. To me, this is no ordinary dream. It is a dream I personally believe God wrote on my heart. Yet, it seems today that this dream will not be realized in my lifetime, and possibly never even in the hereafter.

As I reflect deeper, I know the bottom-line issue with which I am struggling is a matter of faith. I feel that God is calling me to build on my faith, to take my faith to a new level. At this point, I don't know if I'm capable of doing so.

My faith today is built on the belief that whatever challenges I may encounter or whatever unfulfilled hopes and dreams I may have, God will ultimately answer my prayers, in this life or in the life hereafter. With all the injustice and inequality in the world, this is not an easy faith. However, it has always been my faith, and I do the best that I can.

The new level of faith to which God may be calling me is the belief that God is my God, whether or not God will save me or deliver me. I believe I have seen evidence of this faith in scripture.

In the Book of Daniel, it is written that Shadrach, Meshach and Abednego refused to worship the golden statue of King Nebuchadnezzar. As a result, King Nebuchadnezzar threatened to throw the three of them into the fiery furnace to their deaths. Shadrach, Meshach and Abednego answered the king as follows: "If our God whom we serve is able to deliver us from the furnace of blazing fire and out your hand, O King, let him deliver us. But if not, be it known to you, O king, that we will not serve your gods and we will not worship the golden statue that you have set up."

Clearly, Shadrach, Meshach and Abednego believed strongly in God. Their belief in God was not dependent on the expectation that God would deliver them or save them. Also, there is no indication that I can discern that their belief was dependent on life after death. These young men believed in God without condition.

God's promises and assurances to God's people are very real. And that's one thing. But when it comes to faith in God, I ask myself whether God is calling me to hold that faith without condition.

PRAYER: Almighty God, I pray for me and for all of your children. I pray that we might be strong in our faith. I pray that we grow closer to you and to each other and that we each be true to our own individual spiritual journeys. AMEN

Waiting, and Watching

Bridget Melien

IT'S DARK, I'M WAITING, IT'S COLD and I'm questioning everything, but I'm waiting, and watching.

I don't know about you, but the winter months can be particularly challenging for me. Especially after Christmas is over. But I'm waiting, and watching. Winter just seems interminable to me sometimes, the dark and cold, and layers of clothing. The length of time that is still left to go leaves me less motivated to do the many things I love to do. I seem to spend more time alone, which can be good, but can get old too. I'm definitely not outside in the air as much as my body and soul needs. I hibernate, I eat more carbs that I know I should, read endlessly. But I'm waiting, and watching. I'm hauling wood, stoking the stove, making a little cocoon of warmth that I crawl into.

My prayers bring me to this psalm over and over as I am waiting, and watching. *"Create in me a pure heart, O God, and renew a steadfast spirit in me"*. Psalm 51:10

And then, I see it, and I feel it. It's 4:30 and it's still light out and I start obsessing over the minutes we gain each day. I start to perk up. And then it's a warmer day, walking in the woods discovering the witch hazel in bloom. Now I'm really waiting, and watching.

My prayers turn to passages like this one more often. *"I will give you a new heart and put a new spirit within you; I will take the heart of stone out of your flesh and give you a heart of flesh"*. Ezek 36:26

Waiting, and watching for the rebirth that God promises, each and every year. Rebirth and resurrection become my common themes as we approach the Easter season. The promise of eternal life, and the cycles of life over and over, the seasons over and over. *"And this is the promises that He has promised us – eternal life. "* Jn 2:25

The little signs of new life bring me renewed engagement with the world, and even though I know there's a way to go, and that there will be more dark and cold, the seed is planted in my heart. My step is lighter, the birds at the feeder seem jollier, the hellebore is trying to peak out, and I know the promise of spring and the Resurrection is coming.

My final prayer for a bit now: *O Lord, thank you for the everlasting promise of the return of spring and the resurrection of Easter that sustains me through the long dark winter.*

Joyful Noise

Sharon Roundtree-Brewer

*Make a joyful noise unto the Lord, all the earth; make
a loud noise and rejoice, and sing praise.*

Ps 98:4 (KJV)

OVER THE LAST YEAR I HAVE BEEN PLEASED to see so many members of our congregation willing to honor God with their musical talent. I have especially enjoyed the willingness of our youth to share the music they love with us and with God. I would like to share some of my memories of the way music has been a part of my worship and my relationship with God. I have shared this with the congregation before but because I have been inspired by so much of the music in our recent services I am moved again to express my thoughts and feelings about music and worship.

My earliest religious experiences were in the Pentecostal Holiness church of my maternal grandmother. If ANYONE knew how to make a joyful noise it was certainly the congregation of my grandmother's church. It was there at a very early age that I developed my love for the upbeat, uninhibited, wonderfully joyful music that was a part of the services in that church. It was with great excitement that the congregation expressed their love of Jesus and of God. It seemed to me impossible to sit in the pews and NOT feel the Holy Spirit.

The music and spirit of the Pentecostal Holiness church services made such an impression on my young companions and me that during the week following Sunday service, my siblings, my cousins, and I would "play" church as often as we could. My cousin Nate was the preacher and the rest of us were members of the congregation. We sang, we danced, we clapped, and we were filled with the Holy Spirit, just as the adults had been on Sunday morning.

As I grew up and moved away from home, I began attending other churches and these did not include churches of the Pentecostal Holiness denomination. The churches I attended did not worship with the same outward expression of joy I experienced in those early years. I think the only times I experienced the kind of service I remember as a youth was when I would attend services in Georgia at the Baptist church my husband's family attended. I would sit in the pews of the church of my husband's youth and see the same expressions of joy on the faces of the members of that congregation and could not help but be filled with the Holy Spirit. *I* was not jumping and dancing and clapping (that is not my personality), but I could *feel* the Holy Spirit.

Perhaps you have seen the type of worship I am describing in movies or on television. The scenes I recall try to depict a typical Pentecostal or Baptist service similar to the ones that I have experienced. The worship service that is depicted in the media is disappointing because for me the scenes do not capture what is really going on in those services. Actually, there is no way to experience this kind of worship service unless you are there. The musical experience of the Pentecostal tradition was wonderful for me. However, my overall spiritual needs took me into a different direction and to a different kind of church. In my spiritual journey it has been my pleasure to experience all kinds of music in a variety of worship services. Each in its own way has moved me.

My hope is that the members of our congregation will continue to share their gift of music with us and that we will continue to allow others outside of our congregation to come and share their musical gifts. In that sharing we most certainly will strengthen our relationship with God and with each other.

Shout your praises to God, everybody! Let loose and sing! Strike up the band! Round up an orchestra to play for God, Add on a hundred-voice choir. Feature trumpets and big trombones, Fill the air with praises to King God. Let the sea and its fish give a round of applause, With everything living on earth joining in.

Ps 98:4-7 (MSG)

Light is Sweet

Betsy Bascom

Light is sweet,
and it pleases the eye to see the sun.

(ECCL 11:7)

ONE OF MY FAVORITE BOOKS growing up was Laura Ingalls Wilder's *The Long Winter*. I remember my mom reading it to all five of us before bed and falling in love with the perseverance of the characters through such adversity.

I have read it many times since then. That being said, as I write this on the first Sunday in March, I feel as if we have been living through the longest winter ever! I am very tired of feeling cold, shoveling and trudging through snow and ice and living through an abundance of cloudy days. But there is a light at the end of the tunnel.

God's creation is coming alive after such a long sleep. I am witnessing changes every day. The days are getting longer, the streams are running full, daffodils are popping up in a sheltered garden at school, a possum was spotted sitting on the railing of my deck and, most importantly, I am hearing the birds singing early in the morning as I walk down to get my paper.

Yes, the ice flow is still huge and frozen at the bottom of my driveway, the ground is still covered in a blanket of snow and I am still wrapped in layers to keep warm, but the birds are singing their sweet songs. The world is waking up! Praise Be to God!

See! The winter is past;
the rains are over and gone.
Flowers appear on the earth;
the season of singing as come,
The cooing of doves
is heard in our land.

(Song 2:11-12)

In Praise of God's Glorious Creation

A Little Something to Chew On

Karen Bergenholtz

A WHILE BACK THE MIDDLEFIELD FEDERATED CHURCH switched to gluten free bread for communion, and as with many changes it has taken some getting used to. Frequent comments have been made about how long it takes to chew and swallow this different cube of element. And though we may seem more self-conscious of exercising our jaws than we were accustomed to during this time of solitude and communion, we seem to be adapting.

During one of the last communion Sundays it occurred to me, though we may ruminate over the time it takes to consume this changed element, I could simply look at it as a way to spend more time in prayer with God, and less aware of the mechanics of my jaws. What should I be concerned about? Am I spending 5, 10 or 15 more seconds? It turns out this new gluten free option has been a "god-send".

> *"Do not conform any longer to the pattern of this world, but be*
> *transformed by the renewing of your mind. Then you will be able to test*
> *and approve what God's will is —his good, pleasing and perfect will."*

ROM 12:2

Well, today is April 22 as I write this message. Two days after Easter Sunday. The day after the Boston Marathon, 2014. I read in the paper today, a comment from Meb Keflezighi, the winner: "I prayed a lot," he said. "I said, "God, help me get to that finish line. Do it for the people."

Meb ran 26.2 continuous miles in two hours, eight minutes and thirty-seven seconds, asking God to help him. Maybe I can spend some extra time with communion bread.

Two days after Easter Sunday. Good News. God lives. Lots to chew on. Amen

The Tree

Lori Michaud

Some days when I feel wretched and sad as sad can be
I walk until I find myself a simply perfect tree.
The tree is old and gnarled, yet strong and noble still
I wonder, how I wonder, as I sit upon that hill.
Were I that tree, what would I see?
How would I relate to me?
Would every knot annoy me, or every tangled branch?
Would that twisted root below me make my tree bark blanch?
Would I envy every bird of flight and wonder why oh why
Do they have all the fun, while I just touch the sky?
Would I overlook my strength, my great nobility?
Would I diminish all the beasts that love and respect me?
I have a beauty all my own, it's bound up in my soul.
I will embrace it for myself as I sit upon this knoll.
As for that bird, so lovely, flying free as free,
I'm sure he's hyper-focused on a flaw we cannot see.

The Blame Game

Roger Brewer

▲ ▲ ▲

DO YOU LISTEN TO OR WATCH TALK SHOWS that appear on radio or television? Are you a patron of morning or evening news programs? What are you reading in newspapers or online on your computer? Whatever the source, what are people saying today about other people? What is your experience when you attend religious, civic or social meetings? What are you likely to find in most conversations with your neighbors, friends, family members, co-workers, and others with whom you interact on a daily or regular basis?

Obviously, my subject matter in this writing is the 'blame game.' As a society, myself certainly included, we are obsessed with blaming others. The rich blames the poor. The poor blames the rich. The Democrats blame the Republicans. The Republicans blame the Democrats. The 'righteous' blames the 'sinners.' The 'sinners' blame the 'righteous.' The 'natives' blame the foreigners. The foreigners blame the 'natives.' You get picture. We blame anyone who does not act or look like we do. And often, the blame gets very personal and very nasty, indeed. Whatever the subject or situation, it's always the other person's fault.

> The man said, "The woman whom You gave to be with me,
> she gave me from the tree, and I ate." Then the LORD God
> said to the woman, "What is this you have done?" And the
> woman said, "The serpent deceived me, and I ate."

GEN 3:12-13

You may be aware that there are many examples in the Bible, from Genesis and thereafter, of people blaming others for situations in which they find themselves. When we blame other people, what we are doing essentially is judging them. Jesus teaches us, "Do not judge, so that you may not be judged." But this commandment to not judge others does not mean, in my opinion, that we should give up discernment altogether. We must still be discerning of people and situations. However, the extensive blaming of others in society today, especially with the current level of animosity, goes far beyond the discernment that God expects of God's people.

Why then do we spend so much time and energy judging others? Sometimes we hold negative judgment against others for material gain. Our negative judgment influences public opinion and public behavior against our competitors, and thus gives us an advantage in competition with our competitors for economic, political or social gain. Sometimes we judge others in an effort to escape or own personal responsibility, as did Adam and Eve in the Garden of Eden. At other times, we blame others in a foolish effort to address our own feelings of insecurity. When we put others down, we feel good about ourselves.

Whatever the motivation to judge others, it is my belief that blaming others is not a strength, but a weakness.

PRAYER: Almighty God, I pray for us all in our obsession to judge one another. If I am lost or misguided in my point of view, I pray that I might see the light. If I am correct in whole or in part, may we all see the light, and grow stronger and closer to what you expect of your people. Amen.

Personal Weeds

Paul Bergenholtz

I HOPE THAT YOU ARE HAVING A PLEASANT SUMMER. Summer is a time where we slow down a bit, possibly go on vacation and enjoy the beauty of nature. The flowers are in bloom and the fresh fruit and vegetables are all around us to enjoy.

For some, gardening is a favorite summer activity and if you are a gardener, you know that if you are to keep a garden in good shape, it requires a lot of attention, as well as some sweat and hard work. Gardening is enjoyable, but it takes the strong commitment of the gardener to produce a bountiful harvest. Like the gardener, we should also take care of our spiritual life, if we expect to live a life of beauty and bounty. The attentive gardener must always be on the lookout for those nasty and invasive weeds. As Christians, we should be attentive to those "personal weeds" that can grow inside us.

We all have "personal weeds" and do these examples of "personal weeds" sound familiar?

* You have been slighted by someone, maybe by a friend or relative, but you are unwilling to forgive them.
* You are highly critical of others, especially those who do not live up to your standards.
* You jump to conclusions about people and their point of view without actively listening to what they have to say.

These "personal weeds," if left unattended, can strangle our true inner spirit and we can become unsightly before others and our God. Like the diligent gardener, we should always tend to our spiritual well being. That work should never go on vacation.

Have a great summer.

Perfectly Imperfect

Elisabeth Kennedy

I AM A BIT OF A PERFECTIONIST, which isn't always a good thing. If I don't look good enough, I don't want to go out —my dress has to be perfect, my shoes match it perfectly, and my hair, of course, has to look great.

Sometimes I've been afraid to join (a club, a group, etc.) because I think I am not good enough. I am afraid to write, because it won't be perfect. I'm afraid to speak, because I won't do it perfectly—I might cry, I might stutter….

I do the same with my heart. I push away worries; hide my messes, my faults and failures. I avoid conversations, or I simply don't show up at all. *"I'll wait until I have it more together,"* which really means, *"I'll wait until I can do it perfectly."*

My mother used to get angry with me, telling me "If you wait until everything is perfect, you'll never do anything," and even "the day you can do everything perfectly, you'll be dead. Make the most of what God gave you here and now." She's a wise woman, my mother.

It was a hard lesson to learn, and one I'm constantly re-learning. . . God is not asking us to do anything flawlessly, just faithfully. It was in mission work that I learned not *"just do it"* as Nike urges, but *"do your best, and let God do the rest."* That has been such a comfort to me. I've been able to let go of much of that need for perfection. It is not me who has to be perfect – it is God who is perfect.

I still struggled to write this piece, afraid to go out of my comfort zone and admit my fears, and gee – not be perfect…. But I am hoping by doing so

I can encourage other perfectionists out there not to let perfection hold you back, but put your best foot forward and show up, stop hiding and be present. We all need to show up, exactly as we are, because God created each of us to His purpose. If we don't show up and share ourselves and what may seem to us an imperfect talent, that purpose is not fulfilled. That piece of God that is you only gets shared with the world if you show up and share your perfectly imperfect self. Our presence is a present, to God and to each other.

I praise you because I am fearfully and wonderfully
made; your works are wonderful.

Ps 139 (NIV)

Messages from a Watermelon

Valerie Faiella

GOD IS AMAZING! FOR YEARS we have tried to grow flowers and vegetables. The boys and I would buy seeds and begin them in little cups in the early spring. We'd gradually move them to bigger pots where they would grow and eventually . . . die. We tried bigger pots. We tried planting them in the yard. (There is a reason it is called "Rockfall.") Every inch or so is yet another . . . rock. And still nothing. We tried sunny spots, shady spots, and everything in between. I kept encouraging them, hoping they'd see and taste the fruits of their labors. (No pun intended.) Oh, we'd get a few "little" tomatoes that made cherry tomatoes look huge and never turned red. Or, we'd finally get something growing and the local wild life would stop by to thank us for their meal. (I guess our next attempt will be enclosed raised beds.) So, needless to say, we stopped trying a few years back.

You can only imagine our surprise when we noted an errant vine running along the shrubs in the middle of the summer. We decided to let it go and see what developed. To our amazement we now have two watermelons growing and thriving!! What's that saying? "Let go and let God." We let go of thinking we could ever grow anything. Perhaps last summer, watermelon seeds were left behind after eating watermelon, but we did not plant them. We did nothing to cultivate them and magically watermelon appeared. ***God is good!***

- It made me stop to think, "what other areas of my life am I trying so hard to accomplish something on my own and getting nowhere?" (*How about you?*)
- What am I able to do? (*What are you able to do?*) And what can we just allow God to do?
- Do your part and allow God to do His.
- When you shoulder the burden and try to "do-it-all," you don't allow God to reveal what He is more than capable of doing.

> *My job was to plant the seed in your hearts, and Apollos watered it, but*
> *it was God, **not we**, [emphasis added] who made it grow. The ones*
> *who do the planting or watering aren't important, but God is important*
> *because He is the one who makes the seed grow. The one who plants*
> *and the one who waters work as a team with the same purpose . . ."*

1 COR 3:6-8

PRAYER

Thank you Heavenly Father for all the abilities you endowed each one of us with. Thank you too that we were never meant to "do-it-all" on our own.

The Appointed Life

Roger Brewer

FEW WOULD DENY THAT THE CIRCUMSTANCES of our birth determine much about the lives we live. For example, if you are born poor you are likely to live and die poor. Certainly, some do rise above the poverty into which they are born but most do not.

I have heard the suggestion that we as individuals participated (prior to our birth) in deciding our own circumstances of birth. If this is the case, it would be interesting to know why I chose to be born into poverty and apartheid. Indeed, why would anyone choose adverse birth conditions? For sure, I do not have the understanding that some may have on how we decided our own birth. I will try to stay open to a fuller understanding. In the meantime, I choose to believe our birth conditions were determined by God.

I have always believed God determined my gender, race, parents, time of birth, physical body, physical abilities, mental capacity and place of birth. By determining these things, God also determined necessarily the social, political and economic conditions into which I was born. Just to be clear, I do not believe God created war, poverty or other adversities of the world. These things resulted from human behavior. But, in my mind, the birth of some into human-made adversity, when others are born into more favorable conditions, is within the province of the Almighty God.

But why did God give each of us the particular circumstances of birth that we received? Lately, I have been thinking a lot about this question with a heightened sense of appreciation of the dominant role that birth conditions play in the living of our lives.

> *Now the word of the Lord came to [Jeremiah] saying, "Before I formed you in the womb I knew you, and before you were born I consecrated you; I appointed you a prophet to the nations."*

JER 1:4-5

As it was with the prophet Jeremiah, is it not likewise for each and every one of us? Did God know us before we were conceived in the womb, and did God appoint each of us to one or more important causes in life? Obviously, everyone is not appointed prophet to the nations. Nevertheless, does God not appoint each of us to do work that is important to God, even if that work is considered menial or insignificant by human standards?

Many people believe as I do that God speaks to us today in various ways. For example, God speaks to us through the actions and words of others, through nature, through intuition, through dreams, and through the talents and abilities bestowed on us. I also believe God speaks to us profoundly through the circumstances of our birth.

Seeing my birth conditions and the birth conditions of others, not as an advantage or disadvantage, but as the powerful word of the Almighty God is no small matter. This insight, to say the least, is very empowering and enlightening to me.

PRAYER:

Almighty God, I pray that we might all have a fuller understanding and appreciation of how you speak to us through the circumstances of our birth. May we honor and respect your voice as it abides in ourselves and in others, and may we faithfully carry out your word in the living of our lives. AMEN.

What Does Christmas Mean to You?

Bridget Melien

TO ME IT'S MANY THINGS, as I am sure it is with you too: A very special birthday celebration, traditions, family, friends, festive food and drinks, and certainly lots of hustle and bustle.

This year I've spent some time trying to find true personal meaning of the season on a deeper level beyond those I've mentioned above. Making quiet time for myself, reading, meditating and just being. I've been reading a lot of poetry and came across an Emily Dickinson poem that strikes a chord with me about Christmas and hope. It goes like this:

HOPE is the thing with feathers
That perches in the soul.
And sings the time without the words,
And never stops at all.

And sweetest in the gale is heard;
And sore must be the storm
That could abash the little bird
That kept so many warm.

I've heard it in the chilliest land,
And on the strangest sea;
Yeast never in extremity,
It asked a crumb of me

A poem of hope, a birth of hope. Hope for the future, for me and you and for our world. Hope that the next year God and Jesus' love touches lives all around the world. That we fight less and love more, are kinder and gentler to ourselves and others, friends, family and strangers alike.

Christmas has become a season of hope and renewal for me this year and I pray that it does for you as well.

God Bless and Merry Christmas.

*For in this hope we were saved. Now hope that is seen is
not hope. For who hopes for what he sees? But if we hope
or what we do not see, we wait for it with patient.*

ROM 8: 24-25 (NIV)

2015

Happy New Year!
Lori Michaud

▲ ▲ ▲

THE BEGINNING OF JANUARY IS LIKE A CLEAN SLATE—a new calendar, a new start, another chance to be a better you. Nothing has happened to mar this new pristine year yet. Our dreams and plans are still achievable. We have 365 days ahead of us to make those resolutions stick.

What happens, then, around the middle of January? When we tire from the effort of change? When we lose momentum and steam in our pursuits? When everything looks bleak and depressing? The whole year is still ahead of us, and we are already looking at failure? What then?

I like to refer to this passage to get me back on track:

> *You were taught, with regard to your former way of life, to put off your old self, which is being corrupted by its deceitful desires; "to be made new in the attitude of your minds; and to put on the new self, created to be like God in true righteousness and holiness.*

EPH 4:22-24

We are being made new every day. We learn from our setbacks, and then make progress.

We are all in the process of transformation, and each breath we take is another new beginning. As long as we are striving for our goal we are succeeding.

May you allow yourself to be made new in the attitude of your mind. May you accept Gods forgiveness of your shortcomings, and forgive yourself as well. May you remember that every moment is a chance to change, and God is right there with you through it all.

FEBRUARY 1

God's Light

Betsy Bascom

"The people walking in darkness have seen a great light."

ISA 9:2

I DON'T KNOW ABOUT YOU, but I hate getting up in the dark and getting home from work in the dark. I miss the daylight this time of the year. My mother was the same. She would start watching the sunrise and sunset times every day in the paper after the Winter Solstice, a habit I too have adopted. As I write this, we have gained about 30 minutes of daylight since that shortest day of the year. It is comforting and brings me hope.

My Bible defines light as daytime, brightness, illumination, exposure to the truth. Think about it—a bright and constant Light, which will illuminate us with exposure to the truth.

"You, O Lord, keep my lamp burning; My
God tums my darkness into light."

PS 18:28

No more darkness, only the hope that the Light gives us. What a wonderful promise, to arise and live each and every day in a glorious dawn. No more fear, only joy in His presence and Word.

295

*"The Lord is my light and my salvation; whom shall I fear? The
Lord is the stronghold of my life, of whom shall I be afraid?"*

Ps 27:1

There is a Light that is ever present and can be ours for the asking if only we
open our hearts and let Him in.

*"Arise, shine, for your light has come, and the
glory of the Lord rises upon you."*

Isa 60:1

Wishing you the glory of the Light.

Our Abbreviated Lives

Karen Bergenholtz

YOU ALL PROBABLY HAVE ONE. I know I do. Pet peeve? Today I'd like to share one. Everyone most likely experiences this, when the check-out clerk utters, mutters these words: "Have a good one". Walking away, I think, one what? One moment, minute, hour, day, week, month, year, life? Pretty non-specific, those words cover whatever the recipient would like them to.

A few years ago, a common way to end a conversation or transaction was "have a nice day", which for some, replaced the sentiment, "have a good day".

"Have a good day" seems to have evolved from "God give you a good day". Somewhere in time the "God give you" disappeared. The wish, "God give you" is replaced with the command, "Have". A nice, good, day, or one. Whether willing or able, no matter what the day is like, you are to "have" a good _____. It's all up to me.

But if I think to myself, adding the words "God give you" to the senti-ment, I may become mindful of God's presence in my life. Wow! My bold farewell response could be "And may God give you a good day!"

We may feel the need in the rush of our everyday lives, to abbreviate our greetings to each other, emails and texts replace phone calls and the written word. What would the apostle Paul say to our abbreviated manner of commu-nication? I leave you with his good encouragement. "Finally, beloved, what-ever is true, whatever is honorable, whatever is just, whatever is pure, whatever is pleasing, whatever is commendable, if there is any excellence and if there is anything worthy of praise, think about these things. Keep on doing the things that you have learned and received and heard and seen in me, and the God of peace will be with you". Phil 4:8-9

Words to bring encouragement, hope, confidence, and faith in our God, and our mission to build and strengthen relationships with God, one another, and our world.

We Made It!

Lori Michaud

▲ ▲ ▲

THIS WAS ONE LONG AND BRUTAL WINTER! I know most of us were looking ahead to spring with the warming sunshine, singing robins, and blooming flowers… oh, and trees. I forgot about the tree pollen. And seasonal allergies. And the itchy eyes.

So, summer is on its way! I can't wait for beach days, a more relaxed pace, and vacations… oh and the humidity. I almost forgot about the stifling heat. And mosquitos. And the crowds of people at all the fun touristy places.

Well, autumn is coming with its beautiful foliage, crisp air, and apple cider… and mold allergies. And don't forget the pressure of heading back to school. Oh, and let's not forget the holiday prep that starts before Halloween.

Okay, so winter might not be so bad. The snow can be quite beautiful, and it is nice to have time to cuddle up in our houses with our cozy sweaters and blankets. The cold is brutal though, and the snow gets so heavy…and there is such a thing a cabin fever.

No matter where we are in life there are good things and bad things about it. I find it easy to romanticize about the next phase while wallowing in the negatives of the phase I am in currently. I am in a constant state of chasing happiness, imagining that it is just around the corner.

Every week in church I ask God: Thy Kingdom Come, Thy Will be Done, On Earth as it is in Heaven.

Thy Kingdom Come on Earth as it is in heaven. Romans 14:17 Tells us "For the Kingdom of God is not food and drink but righteousness and peace and joy in the Holy Spirit." The Kingdom of God is righteousness and peace and joy in the Holy Spirit. Really? Peace and joy in the Holy Spirit? I think with a mindset change that might actually be obtainable.

I don't want to spend my life wishing away my present. At the risk of sounding like a toddler, I want happiness now. And God says I can have it. All I need to do is shift my focus from the negative to the positive. Focus on the awe inspiring and amazing things around me instead of the tedious drudgery. A shift in mindset can shift my whole life experience. Easy, right?

Not really… It will take a willful effort to catch myself when I am wishing for the next stage to hurry up and get here already. I will need to be mindful to pause and acknowledge all the good that is around me. So my daily prayer will be: God, Help me to see you in every moment, because I truly want to live in peace and joy in you.

Now I will make sure to stock up on allergy medicine and enjoy that warm sunshine on my face. May you all have a fantastic spring!

Peace and Joy be yours.

When Have You Witnessed Courage?

Paul Bergenholtz

▲ ▲ ▲

MANY PEOPLE BELIEVE A "COURAGEOUS ACT" is something performed by others in dangerous situations - a fireman rescues a child from a burning building, a soldier puts their life on the line for others, etc. However, there are other forms of courage that are more subtle and mostly overlooked. What then, is courage?

The Random House Dictionary defines "courage" as "the ability to face difficulty or danger with firmness and without fear." I struggle with the inclusion of "without fear" in Random House's definition, since "fear" is often present when we face difficult situations.

I prefer Webster's definition of "courage" as "the ability to do something that you know is difficult or dangerous." Webster's definition of "courage" implies by its omission of the phrase "without fear" that "fear" may indeed be present. However, it is in spite of our "fear" that we rise to the occasion and do what is "difficult" or perhaps even "dangerous."

Acts of courage are all around us, but they mostly go unnoticed and are often performed without much fanfare. As we become more observant, we may find courage in unexpected places, as I did last summer.

My wife, Karen and I were taking a brief vacation to New York's Hudson Valley and decided to visit the home of President Martin Van Buren. What I observed there both surprised and initially made me a bit uncomfortable.

Our docent/guide had a severe stutter and it took her, for what appeared to be an eternity, to pronounce certain words. Why would someone with a severe speech impediment want a job where the primary requirement is to speak to strangers all day? However upon reflection, I found that I had witnessed "courage" in its purest form, an individual's ability to face difficulties every day, in front of strangers and for all to see.

So what "difficult situations" are you facing? Is it a severe life challenge or a lack of confidence in yourself and your abilities? Like the example of the docent, look for those subtle "acts of courage," find strength in them and be guided by the words found in Joshua 1:9:

"Have I not commanded you? Be strong and of good courage; be not frightened, neither be dismayed; for the Lord your God is with you wherever you go."

Worry (II)
Elisabeth Kennedy

> *"Therefore I tell you, do not worry about your life, what you will eat*
> *or drink; or about your body, what you will wear. Is not life more*
> *than food, and the body more than clothes? Look at the birds of the*
> *air; they do not sow or reap or store away in barns, and yet your*
> *heavenly Father feeds them. Are you not much more valuable than*
> *they? Can any one of you by worrying add a single hour to your life?"*

MT 6:25-27

I CONFESS TO WORRYING. . . especially throughout Richard's illness, and perhaps even more after he died. How would I make it alone? How would I pay all the bills, how would I keep the house…

And, as scripture tells us, not a bit of that worrying added a single hour to my life, or lessened any of my concerns. It was when I finally surrendered to God that I realized that the things I was holding on to truly don't matter. A house is a shell -- it is the people that you put in it that make it a home. Living there alone was not the house I'd enjoyed, it became a burden greater than I need to bear. Also through prayer I have realized that I need not worry about my future.

"For I know the plans I have for you," declares the Lord, "plans to
prosper you and not to harm you, plans to give you hope and a future."

JER 29:11 (NIV)

I am grateful for that hope and finally look forward to the future. I do not know exactly what that will look like, but I am no longer worrying. I know God is with me, and I am filled with hope. I have put my house on the market, I will no longer store away myself and my possessions, but spread my wings and hopefully His love from here to Haiti and I don't know where in between.

I am grateful for my church, for Pastor and so many others who have helped me throughout the challenging years of Richard's illness and especially after his passing. I will continue to visit, and you will forever be in my heart and my prayers.

Thank you, Father, for Your love and grace that exceed our understanding, for the hope that springs eternal, and a future filled with the promise of serving and loving You.

JULY 1

Awe

Valerie Faiella

AWE: AN OVERWHELMING FEELING OF REVERENCE, admiration, fear, etc. produced by that which is grand, sublime, extremely powerful, or the like. (Dictionary.com)

When was the last time you were: In "awe" of something? Or "awe-inspired" by something? Or struck with an overwhelming sense of reverence or admiration? How many things are so commonplace in your life that you've lost the "awe" or "admiration" in them? How many miracles take place in your daily life that you don't even recognize? Does this happen in your devotionals too?

Next time you are with a small child, observe the awe of that child discovering a beautiful flower. A Flower you may have passed right, by without a second glance. Consider that! A seed, usually smaller than your pinky fingernail, and it gives way to become a beautiful flower. Something full of color, a scent, layers and layers of petals!! Really, a miracle and yet we see them so often that their magnificence is lost.

I'm sorry to say that sometimes, I find myself listening to scripture, or reading it, and think, "I know this story". I have heard it so many times that is has "lost" its "awe". Can you imagine Exodus 15:8: *"By the blast of your nostrils the waters piled up. The surging waters stood up like a wall; the deep waters congealed in the heart of the sea."* Pause for a moment and *really* try to imagine walking through a surging SEA of water with the walls rising up on either side of you and seeing what? All kinds of fish? Sharks? Right there!! And NO

Plexiglas in between you or them! Imagine that! And you walk through it! That would be "awe-some," (probably not to mention a bit scary, wondering when, or if, it would come cascading down). I have tremendous reverence for the sea, its power, and the God who created it.

Or how about Jesus in Gethsemane? We usually read about his betrayal at least once a year. If you are like me, you may have glossed over the miraculous healing right in the middle of it!! Luke 22:50-51: *"And one of them struck the servant of the high priest, cutting off his right ear. But Jesus answered, "No more of this!" And he touched the man's ear and healed him."* The servant's ear is cut off!! Can you imagine the work it would take a surgeon today to reattach an ear! (Never mind anesthesia, pre-op clearance, insurance pre-approval, etc.!) In one sentence, as though it happened every day, it states, "He touched his ear, and healed him." WOW!! That's incredible.

If you've been like me and taking your surroundings; the people in your life; or your Bible readings for granted - *please* try at least several times in the upcoming week to really "see" something again for the "first" time. Be awe-inspired!

Bible verses from the NIV Adventure Bible that MFC gives to the 3rd grade class each year

One

Roger Brewer

LATELY, I HAVE BEEN REFLECTING ON THE BELIEF that all of humankind is but ONE. Certainly, this idea of many being ONE is not new to Christians. The Apostle Paul teaches us, "… so we, who are many, are one body in Christ, and individually we are members one of another." (Romans 12:5) Obviously, the Apostle Paul is referring to those who believe in Christ. But if we are one body in Christ, are we not also one body in all of humankind? I believe God's love extends to all of God's children. Does not the oneness of humankind also extend to all, without regard to religious belief or whether one even holds a religious belief at all?

Marianne Williamson writes in her book, *A Year of Miracles: Daily Devotions and Reflections* (Day 185), "On the spirit level, there is no place where you stop and I start. Like waves in the ocean or sunbeams to the sun, there is no real separation. Separation does not actually exist, for there is only one of us here."

Of course, if we see ourselves as ONE, we have no one but ourselves to blame for what's wrong in our lives and that could be very frightening. In addition, if all of humankind is ONE, what we *do* to others we *do* to ourselves. When we love and respect others, we love and respect ourselves. When we include others, accept others without judgment, provide for others in need, we do the same to ourselves. And likewise, when we hate, kill, injure or judge others, or when we harbor prejudice or anger against others, or when we fail to assist others in need, we do the same to ourselves.

We read in Matthew 25:31-46 that when we provide for others in need, we do the same for our Lord, Jesus. And likewise, when we fail or refuse to provide for others in need, we do the same to Jesus. Considering that what we do to others is what we do to Jesus, I do not struggle at all with the belief that what we do to others is also what we do to ourselves.

When we fail to help those in need or fall short of our calling to treat everyone with total dignity and respect, we expose ourselves to conflict and unrest within our society that negatively impacts us all. We retard our development as a humanity and distance ourselves from our God. We destroy ourselves at the very core of who and what we are.

We harbor the illusion that we are harming others, as dictated by our fear, pride or whatever, when in fact there are no "others" to harm. As Williamson writes, "For there is only one of us here." Sometimes when you look quietly and preciously, without judgment, into the eyes of a fellow human being, you can see that it is so.

Some may believe this whole thing about "many being ONE" is only a matter of speaking metaphorically. But for me, and for others for sure, our belief is *not* a metaphor. It is a knowing, not based on material proof or human reasoning, but arising instead out of the heart.

PRAYER: *Almighty God, I pray that you be with us always as we continue to grow in our humanity and our faith. Help us to be strong and unafraid, correctible when we go astray, and completely open and faithful to your guidance and never-ending love.*

Happy New Year! (II)

Bridget Melien

And he who was seated on the throne said, "Behold, I am making all things new." Also he said, "Write this down, for these words are trustworthy and true."

REV 21:5

HAPPY NEW YEAR? REALLY? YUP 59 years old and the end of August still feels like a new year to me. Anticipation for all the things that start anew come September: school, church activities, fall sports, harvest time.

I like the idea of two New Years. It's good for me to have a reset partway through the year. A time that I reflect on my early goals of the year, readjust and recommit. What were your New Year's resolutions? Is it time to revisit them? Sometimes I realize my goals for this year need modifying in one way or another. Perhaps some were too lofty, or some were less of a reach than I should have expected of myself. The one goal I always know needs very little adjusting is my desire for a deepening relationship with God. But even so I take it out, turn it around and examine from all sides. My New Year's resolutions in September this year are to:

Spend more time in prayer
Be kind, be loving

Give myself a break, in all things
Dive deep into MFC activities and ministries

What about you? Do you look at this time of year as a time of renewal and recommitment? What are your New Year's resolutions?

Dear God – Let me hear your voice, let me follow your words, in all I do and all I say as this New Year begins. Amen

Atheists, Christians, SBNRs, and YPTLHs

Sharon Roundtree-Brewer

▲ ▲ ▲

A FEW YEARS AGO, I attended a conference at which the pastor who was the keynote speaker skewered people who described themselves as "Spiritual But Not Religious" (SBNR). She criticized these people exclaiming that they were all about themselves, the so-called "me" generation. She said that the SNRBs proclaim that they can find God everywhere and that they do not need to go to church. She implied that they are anti-social and don't believe in community. I must say that I was uncomfortable with this characterization of SBNRs, because I have often used that same phrase to describe myself, "I'm spiritual but not religious." But what this pastor hears when someone says this to her is not what *I* mean when I say this to someone. I mean that my relationship with God and being a loving spirit are what I want to define me, not my religion's doctrine or dogma.

Also, a few years ago I attended a service at another church and the pastor began the sermon recounting a conversation that he recently had with someone who labeled himself an atheist and as such he did not believe in God. As this pastor got into further conversation with the man, the man described the god he didn't believe in as judgmental, vengeful, and harsh. The pastor then said, "I told this man, I don't believe in that god either."

And believe it or not, more times than I care to count, I have been in situations where I have been asked if I'm a Christian. I used to say yes without any hesitation. Lately however, I'm more inclined to say, "It depends on your definition of Christian or the criteria you are using to define Christian."

If someone were to ask me if I am a "this" or a "that" or an YPTLH (*You Put The Label Here*) I now know that I have to question the questioner and ask him or her "What's your definition of *that* or what criteria do you use to define a person as *this?*"

Here is what I believe: We should be more careful about how we label people and the conclusions we jump to when a person is a self-described YPTLH or other people describe her as such. We need to communicate with each other on a deeper level and have fewer superficial conversations about who we are and what we believe. We need to stop invalidating other people's experiences simply because what they have experienced is not our experience. And, just as we shouldn't label and prejudge a person by his or her physical appearance or ethnicity, or economic status, we shouldn't label and prejudge a person by any tag that society might place on him or her.

Prayer

Please God, let me behave, as I believe.

God's Eyes

Karen Bergenholtz

DO YOU REMEMBER THE SIMPLE craft you may have made as a child, wrapping yarn in varying colors around crossed sticks? We know them as "God's Eyes".

If you research the craft, it traditionally originates from the Huichol people of Mexico, and the creations are known as Sikuli, representing "the power to see and understand things unknown". They may be offered to gods for favor and/or protection. The idea of representing *our God* seeing us all and watching over us is how we may understand the symbol.

I recall the "God Eye" as a result of thinking about the hymn "Be Thou My Vision" recently. My thoughts were prompted by how each of us has differing views on various subjects: politically, socially, culturally, scripture, you name it.

I believe the hymn is more about our desire to have God be our "best thought", "in me dwelling", "mine inheritance", "first in my heart", "my treasure", "heart of my own heart, whatever befall", than for God to be watching us.

It is a prayer *each* of sing, beseeching God to be *our* light.

I pray to see through God's eyes, each of us, in our unique human forms, with all of our diverse human experiences, as created by God, worthy of respect, dignity, and love.

DECEMBER 1

God Is With You

Lori Michaud

How long, Lord? Will you forget me forever?
How long will you hide your face from me?
How long must I wrestle with my thoughts
and day after day have sorrow in my heart?
How long will my enemy triumph over me?
Look on me and answer, Lord my God.
Give light to my eyes, or I will sleep in death,
and my enemy will say, "I have overcome him,"
and my foes will rejoice when I fall.
But I trust in your unfailing love;
my heart rejoices in your salvation.
I will sing the Lord's praise,
for he has been good to me.

Ps 13

THIS TIME OF YEAR CAN BE MAGICAL; full of the joyful anticipation for Christmas and the promise it holds. This time of year can also be isolating, lonely, and exhausting. The most freeing thing I can tell you is God is going to meet you wherever you are. God is with you when you are at your highest and happiest moments in life, and God is there with you in the lowest, most

314

trying moments of your life. God understands and allows us to rail at him like a small child—frustrated, angry, and hurt… and he holds us in his lap and strokes our hair until we cry it out. God doesn't need us to hold it together all the time. If you doubt that, take some time to peruse the book of Psalms. The 7+ class has been exploring the book of Psalms this fall and talking about all the feelings conveyed through the passages. What we have discovered is that there is a wide range of emotions in the book of Psalms, from despair right on through joyful and God is present through it all.

May you feel and know God's presence this Advent season. May you have the courage to turn to the Lord in the difficult moments, and may you remember to share your joyful moments, too. May you give yourself permission to feel whatever you are feeling—no guilt for feeling overwhelmed with blessings and joy, no shame for feeling overwhelmed with loss and grief. You are not alone and you are loved regardless of where you are emotionally. God is with you through it all.

2016

▲▲▲

A New Year

Paul Bergenholtz

WE HAVE JUST JOURNEYED THROUGH ADVENT and celebrated the birth of our Lord and Savior, Jesus Christ. I hope everyone had a Merry Christmas, but we know that the holidays are not always as merry as we wish and sometimes can be downright stressful. In 2015, domestic and global events added to our stress. It appears we are helpless to change the world around us for the better. What is a person to do?

Let me take you back to Sunday, November 22, 2015, which was Christ the King Day, the last Sunday in the Christian calendar. On this Sunday, the Pastor asked the congregation the following question (and I paraphrase): "What is one prayer that you would have for the Advent season this year for you, for the community, for the world? What is one prayer that you would lift up to Christ this season?

The responses coming from the congregation were:

Peace
Forgiveness
Tolerance for all of us
Respect of others opinions
Open our hearts and minds
Acknowledgment of our humanness
Elimination of jealousy and mistrust replaced by love

When you read these prayers from the congregation, they mirror the instruction that Jesus proclaims in Mark 12:29-31:

> *"The most important one," answered Jesus, "is this: 'Hear, O Israel:*
> *The Lord our God, the Lord is one. Love the Lord your God with*
> *all your heart and with all your soul and with all your mind and*
> *with all your strength.' The second is this: 'Love your neighbor*
> *as yourself' There is no commandment greater than these."*

(NIV)

The beginning of a new year offers us the opportunity to reflect how we can change lives for the better. We may not be able to change the world, but we can change how we act in it. We can resolve to be kinder, more respectful, more forgiving, more tolerant and more loving of one another.

This is my hope and prayer.

Clay

Elisabeth Kennedy

"Yet, oh Lord you are our Father. We are the clay, you
are the potter; we are all the work of your hand."

ISA 64:8

THIS SCRIPTURE IS SO MEANINGFUL TO ME. I love the imagery of the potter working the clay, first preparing it by removing impurities that might cause the pot to crack, then cutting, pounding, kneading it before it is placed on the wheel to take the potter's proposed shape. Finally it is fired in high temperatures to produce a strong, usable vessel.

The analogy is meaningful to me. None of us are perfect. It is Our Father who removes our impurities through His forgiveness. His loving kindness smooths out the rough edges, and the storms of life "fire" us into stronger vessels. It reassures me in times of struggle, pain or difficult circumstances that my Father is pounding out my impurities, kneading and molding me into the shape He created for me, and that fire storm is making me a strong, usable vessel.

Certainly undergoing the process of being molded is not always pleasant or comfortable, but it is always worth it. It is a comfort to me to know in times of sorrow, fearing uncertainty that God is working to mold me into the servant He created me to be.

"Change my heart, oh God;
make it ever true.
Change my heart, oh God,
may I be like you.

You are the potter,
I am the clay.
mold me and make me
this is what I pray."

—EDDIE ESPINOSA

Heavenly Father, thank you for caring so much for us that you take the loving care to mold us, shape us, and support us to become stronger vessels to bring your love and light to others. We praise you!

Hang in There

Valerie Faiella

I USE DEVOTIONALS TO GUIDE MY QUIET TIME with God each morning. They guide me through various Bible passages and generally "speak" to me in some way. Many seem to "hit the nail on the head" for what I am (or someone close to me) is going through. The following copyrighted passage (reprinted with permission*) is one I believe may speak to many of you as you are going through your daily routine. You may find, like I do, that some days, or stretches of time, you feel like you are on a treadmill doing "something" but really getting nowhere. Hang in there. May your sense of purpose return to you with renewed enthusiasm.

Purpose in Routine
1 Corinthians 9:26 "I run with purpose in every step."

A rolling-ball clock in the British Museum struck me as a vivid illustration of the deadening effects of routine. A small steel ball traveled in grooves across a tilted steel plate until it tripped a lever on the other side. This tilted the plate back in the opposite direction, reversed the direction of the ball and advanced the clock hands. Every year, the steel ball traveled some 2,500 miles back and forth, but never really went anywhere.

It's easy for us to feel trapped by our daily routine when we can't see a larger purpose. The apostle Paul longed to be effective in making the gospel of Christ know. "I do not run like someone running aimlessly; I do not fight like a boxer beating the air" (1 Cor 9:26 NIV). Anything can become monotonous — traveling, preaching, teaching, and especially being confined in prison. Yet Paul believed he could serve Christ his Lord in every situation.

Routine becomes lethal when we can't see a purpose in it. Paul's vision reached beyond any limiting circumstance because he was in the race of faith to keep going until he crossed the finish line. By including Jesus in every aspect of his life, Paul found meaning even in the routine of life. And so can we.

Lord, give us renewed vision and energy to pursue the goal of making Christ known in the midst of our daily routine.

Jesus can transform our routine into meaningful service for Him.

APRIL 1

Companions

Roger Brewer

SCRIPTURE TEACHES US, "FOR THE love of money is a root of all kinds of evil." (1 Timothy 6:10) Personally, I would go a bit deeper. Pride is a root of all kinds of evil. Certainly, money contributes to Pride, but Pride itself is the dominant cause, in my opinion, of conflict in our society today. When you feel you're better than others and treat them accordingly, conflict ensues. When others feel they're better than you and treat you accordingly, conflict ensues. As a result, we have conflict between individuals, groups, communities, races, religions and nations.

How interesting it is that Pride plays such a dominant role in our lives.

> *"Know ye that the Lord he is God: it is he that hath made us, and*
> *not we ourselves; we are his people and the sheep of his pasture."*

Ps 100:3 (KJV)

But to what extent do we beat our drums falsely or wrongly judge others inferior based on status or achievement or the lack thereof. For sure, we all have a responsibility to work hard with what we have been given in life. Some of us do. Some of us do not. Nevertheless, it was not through our own strength or discretion, but through the generosity of the Almighty God that we were born into certain conditions at the time and place of our birth. Not of our own doing, but through the gift of God we have certain gifts and talents or the lack thereof. We are where we are today in our society largely, if not entirely, through the grace of God. Certainly, if God had done otherwise in providing our birth circumstances and gifts and talents, life for each of us would be entirely different.

But there is a reckoning of all things. Mary Luti, pastor, long-time seminary educator, and UCC devotional writer, recently wrote, "We're dying companions." She wrote further, "For everyone in the great crowd of mortals, age to age, it's the same. Soon I will die with you and you with me."

Think of all the pride, judgment, and self-judgment that occupy our lives today and cause so much hurt, conflict, anxiety, struggle, and war. Are these things that we worship nothing but illusions. If they are not illusions, if in fact they are real, they certainly do not prevail.

Please pray with me the prayer offered up by Mary Luti, *"Life is short, most holy God. Make me tender towards my dying companions, all of us your passing guests."*

What's your Quiet Score?

Bridget Melien

DO YOU MAKE TIME FOR BEING QUIET? I often find it challenging in the day to day of my busy life. I realized recently how much of the day I was ingesting something, books, music, social media, my laptop at work, conversation. It's a lot. And I'm not suggesting that it's all bad, I love the conversations I have with my family and friends. But it is constant and I don't think I realized how taxing on my system it was becoming. I was feeling pretty overwhelmed at times.

Very early in the morning, while it was still dark, Jesus got up, left
the house and went off to a solitary place, where he prayed

Mk 1:35 NIV

Jesus made conscious decisions throughout his life to remove himself from the hustle and bustle and go to a quiet place. The teachings suggest he craved the quiet, to be in prayer and relationship with God. I too realized I craved the quiet and began a small practice. It has had its challenges, but the rewards have far outweighed the challenges. I still have a tendency to want to reach for my phone, but it's getting better.

I wanted to create quiet opportunities to discover and listen for God's presence in my life. Each of us can create a practice of quiet in our own way. There are no set rules; you set what works for you. Maybe it's just removing your phone for a time, going for a walk, working in your garden, meditating. I have a very noisy life and there's a lot of talking and listening to talking. I actually turn off and almost hide my phone, no radio, no TV or streaming and as little talking as I can manage on as many Saturdays as I can manage.

What I have discovered along the way is that the quiet has created the space and time for me to be in a closer relationship with God. I talk to him, share my joys and concerns, and recognize him and all the ways he is working in my life and in the world.

So have some fun, unplug and create some quiet time in your life, and I hope if you do you'll enjoy it as much as I have.

> *"The best remedy for those who are afraid, lonely or unhappy is to go outside, somewhere where they can be quiet, alone with the heavens, nature and God. Because only then does one feel that all is as it should be."*

ANNE FRANK

Don't Drop the Baby

Sharon Roundtree-Brewer

ONE OF THE MOST DIFFICULT TASKS for me each day is trying to maintain a calm and peace inside when there is chaos and turbulence raging outside. I'm not only referring to the chaos in my immediate surroundings but also the chaos in the larger world. How does one maintain a sense of peace and balance when there are so many things (large and small) that can disrupt that peace and balance? For years I have used some scripture that has been very helpful, but a couple of years ago I came across something else that I also use to maintain my equilibrium.

There is an essay in *A Deep Breath of Life*, a book of daily inspirations by Alan Cohen, titled "Don't Drop the Baby." In that essay Cohen uses a quote by Hugh Prather, another writer of inspirational books, in which he compares the peace of God to an infant:

> *If you were carrying a little baby you would make that child your first priority. If someone bumped into you on the street, you wouldn't just drop the baby to follow the person and yell at him. And if your car broke down, you wouldn't abandon the child as you walked to get help. In the same way, we cannot afford to put the peace of God aside for any worldly distraction. The peace of God is more valuable than anything the world has to offer, and we must protect it as consistently as a tender infant.*

The essay and the quote by Hugh Prather gave me a tool that quickly brings me back to peace and balance whenever the tendency to "lose it" occurs. I simply say to myself "don't drop the baby!" It works every time.

Come to me, all you that are weary and are carrying heavy burdens,
and I will give you rest. Take my yoke upon you, and learn from
me; for I am gentle and humble in heart, and you will find rest
for your souls. For my yoke is easy, and my burden is light.

Mt 11:28-30

Prayer: May you find a way or two to keep the peace of God inside of you whenever those difficult times arise, be they small or life changing. Amen

A Reminder
Karen Bergenholtz

I COULDN'T SEE HIS FACE:
I couldn't see his face – the driver in the left turning lane while waiting for the light to turn green. Both our windows were open, my radio was turned to a news program, reports continuing about Orlando, and music played from the other car. I reached for my camera hoping to capture what was in my visual field but the green light appeared, and we continued on separate ways.

Here's what I hoped to capture: first, a cross, hanging from the rear-view mirror, pewter color on a metal chain; the driver's right hand, folded over the steering wheel, confident, relaxed, strong; the right arm, stretched out, with only the forearm visible, again, exhibiting confidence, relaxed, strong.

I couldn't see the face—but the snapshot was perfectly framed—hand on the wheel—the cross a reminder of faith—confident, relaxed, in charge.

At times we are given small comforts, reassurances, whether it be a word from a friend, a writing, a message, a song or image. At times we need these little "signs", if only as a prompt, a nudge, a reminder. The image was what I needed that day. And here is a little "Christmas in July" for you, words from Henry Wadsworth Longfellow:

I heard the bells on Christmas day
Their old familiar carols play,
And wild and sweet the words repeat
Of peace on earth, good will to men.

I thought how, as the day had come,
The belfries of all Christendom
Had rolled along th'unbroken song
Of peace on earth, good will to men.

And in despair I bowed my head:
'There is no peace on earth,' I said
'For hate is strong, and mocks the song
Of peace on earth, good will to men.'

Then pealed the bells more loud and deep:
'God is not dead, nor doth He sleep;
The wrong shall fail, the right prevail,
With peace on earth, good will to men.'

Till, ringing, singing on its way,
The world revolved from night to day
A voice, a chime, a chant sublime,
Of peace on earth, good will to men.

Changes

Lori Michaud

I FEEL A LITTLE BIT LIKE I DID the summer before I started college. It's bittersweet, saying goodbye to the familiar and looking with excitement (and a little fear) towards the new experiences we have ahead of us. Change is uncomfortable to say the least, and my emotions around facing a pastoral change are wildly mixed.

It helps to know that we will be facing this new adventure together. We will be working together to further define our goals as a church. We have an idea of what we want to do through our mission: *With the help of the Holy Spirit, our mission is to build and strengthen relationships with God, one another, and our world.*

This last year has brought new programs and life to some areas of our church—like truly opening our doors to nonprofit organizations who represent our mission, the 3rd Sunday program, the hugely successful Food Truck Night, and our choir's strong representation at Middlefield's 150th celebration. Our Missions to MFC and our garden team who revitalized the indoor garden area have given us a beautiful space to worship, all while fulfilling our church mission. We are on a good course. We now have an opportunity to adjust our sails, and hopefully a new wind can take us farther than we ever imagined.

May God guide us through the months ahead. May we have the courage and the strength to examine our church and celebrate the positives, be honest about our shortcomings, and be open to new possibilities. May we continue to support each other, learn more about ourselves, and grow from the changes we face together.

Deacons from 2003 to 2016

▲ ▲ ▲

Bascom, Betsy (2005-2015)
Bergenholtz, Karen (2003-present)
Bergenholtz, Paul (2008-present)
Brewer, Roger (2003-present)
Carlin, Barb (2006-2007; 2012)
Crompton, Chuck (2005)
Faiella, Valerie (2013-present)
Galgowski, Dorothy (2008)
Herrington, Patti (2004-2005)
Kennedy, Elisabeth (2013-present)
Kennedy, Richard (2003-2012)
Melien, Bridget (2008-present)
Michaud, Lori (2012-present)
O'Sullivan, Beth (2004-2011)
Piddock, Claire (2005-2007)
Roundtree-Brewer, Sharon (2003-present)
Satagaj, Michael (2010-2014)
Simonzi, Millie (2004-present)
VanDerzee, Sue (2003-2006)
Waller, Dorothy (2003-2005)
Waller, Michael (2006-2010)
Wimler, Deb (2007)
Wolfgang, Gordon (2007-2010)

Index to Reflections

▲ ▲ ▲

34441161R00211

Made in the USA
Middletown, DE
21 August 2016